T0209275

boundless

also by the author

Novels
Annabel

Short Fiction
boYs
The Freedom in American Songs

boundless

TRACING LAND AND DREAM IN
A NEW NORTHWEST PASSAGE

kathleen winter

COUNTERPOINT
BERKELEY

Library of Congress Cataloging-in-Publication Data Is Available

ISBN 978-1-61902-798-5

COUNTERPOINT
2560 Ninth Street, Suite 318
Berkeley, CA 94710
www.counterpointpress.com

Printed in the United States of America

FOR JD

contents

Northwest Passage

ELLESMERE ISLAND

CROKER BAY
DUNDAS HARBOUR
DEVON ISLAND
MELVILLE ISLAND
BATHURST ISLAND
BEECHEY ISLAND
PRINCE LEOPOLD ISLAND
BANKS ISLAND
PRINCE OF WALES ISLAND
FALSE STRAIT
McClintock Channel
PASLEY BAY
Prince Regent Inlet
VICTORIA ISLAND
KING WILLIAM ISLAND
KUGLUKTUK
Coronation Gulf
GJOA HAVEN
JENNY LIND ISLAND
PORT EPWORTH
BATHURST INLET

News

GREENLAND

Baffin Bay

UPERNAVIK

KARRAT FJORD

ILULISSAT

KANGERLUSSUAQ

Davis Strait

BYLOT ISLAND

POND INLET

SISIMIUT

BAFFIN ISLAND

Foxe Basin

"Water, land, wind, sky — these are the only
ones with absolute freedom."
— BERNADETTE DEAN

❧

"The body is a feather blown across the tundra."
— AAJU PETER

chapter one

AN INVITATION

A WEEK BEFORE I got the invitation that would revive an old, lost search of mine, I lay on a dock with college friends. This was our second summer reunion after thirty years of going on with our separate lives, and we'd all grown up. I'd turned fifty and could finally laugh with a kind of compassion at the heartbreakingly young faces of our yearbook photos. We'd forgiven petty old hurts and now saw each other with more far-sighted, more human eyes. I wasn't used to the laughter — I was used to long hours squirrelled away in a room, alone, writing, then my family coming home for supper; once in a while, a foray out to the library or to have coffee with one friend at a time, or a short pilgrimage alone. This was a dock party. I felt like a character in a Judy Blume book. We had cold beer and nachos, and the cottage was a scrap of heaven that Aloise, my old university roommate, had built with her husband.

Lying on that dock I remembered how many questions I'd had about life back when Aloise and I lived together as students, in a tenement above a tavern that pulsed coloured light into my bedroom. In those days I sensed, at times, a transformation of the ordinary world, catching a glimpse of something beautiful and strange. The glimpse transformed stones, apples, streets, and trees into something other than a storyless chaos: I saw the city bathed in a kind of inaudible music, or swirling transparence, with mysterious significance. In those moments, there was no such thing as ordinary. When the glimpse vanished, as it always did, I was bereft. I felt the world had been trying to speak. The whole of existence felt charged with a luminous significance about which I yearned to know more.

Throughout my youth these transcendent events plunged me, for a few minutes at a time, into a blaze of connectedness and belonging. It was as if I were a lost piece of energy — as if sometimes, for an instant of bliss, I accidentally got connected to the electrical circuit to which I'd belonged all along. But then the disconnection recurred, and the familiar sadness. The vision I glimpsed in those blazing moments was powerful and alive, but it was, too, mysteriously imperilled. Something told me that this life, with its simple, dear things — cranes against the skyline, dawn light on gulls' wings, and the loveliness of light and shadow on city staircases — this life was more than it seemed, and it was endangered in a way I did not yet understand. I asked others if they felt this, I studied my college texts to see if they could explain, and I searched spiritual paths as well; but the only real source was the natural world itself, its tangible objects, its light, and its forms.

I did find company in poets, who seemed to me to be the only people who understood. William Wordsworth wrote that in his youth, the earth and "every common sight" appeared to him clothed in light, with "the glory and freshness of a dream." But having grown older, he lamented, "Nothing can bring back the hour / Of splendour in the grass, of glory in the flower..." I knew what he meant. After I left university my own perception dwindled to make room for the details of what my daughters would call my "homesteading phase." I wandered into marriage with a man who hoped I was someone I could never be. He fell ill and after two years he died, and sometimes I thought he'd died of disappointment in me. We had a little girl and after her father died she helped me stack wood and clean the chimney, standing under it with a bucket into which I, with a steel brush on the roof, swept the soot.

Then I met my second husband, a bricklayer, stone worker, and chimney expert, and things began to look up. We had a second daughter and got caught up in the work of raising a family. In that world, though there were beautiful times, that old, mysterious vision, or lost world, retreated behind soup pots and mortgage payments and feeding our goats. I quietly despaired of finding any key to the world I'd glimpsed just underneath—or somehow within—this ever-so-uninspired one.

But now that phase had neared its end. We'd moved to Montreal and I'd left my chimney brush behind. My daughters were becoming more independent and I could come here, to Aloise's lake, with the old friends who'd surrounded me in my youth, when everything was all about possibility. Lying in the sun as waves lapped the dock, I became my younger and older selves at the same time.

Every now and then one of us would blurt something we'd learned over the years, and it was Denise who said, "One thing I've learned is, always be ready to accept an invitation if it means you get to travel somewhere. If anyone says to me, 'Denise, wanna go skiing in the Rockies?' or if they say, 'Hey, four of us were gonna go see Scarlett Johansson on Broadway but Hadley can't make it now,' do you know what I say?"

"No, Denise," I said. "What do you say?"

"My. Bags. Are. Already. Packed."

"Wow."

"And I mean it. I have a packed bag in my closet that's always ready to go. It has a pared-down version of my toiletries, underwear, a couple of changes of clothes. I don't even need to look in it."

I loved this idea. I wasn't sure if it was because I was lying, sun-warmed, on the silvery boards of Aloise's dock in July — little slaps of the wavelets lulling me, then a loon call, and puffy white clouds sailing by — but I felt a thrill.

"I'll do it too," I said. "I'm gonna pack my getaway bag as soon as I get home."

"Don't just talk about it," Denise said, sucking on her beer with that same mischief she'd had thirty years before. Denise was an instigator. She was the one who dared you to spill your secrets, but she never spilled any of her own. She was a wicked woman and I felt some of her subversiveness rub off on me as I imagined packing my getaway case and stashing it in my bedroom closet.

"Don't clutter it up with too much stuff," she warned. "The bare necessities. That's the key. Don't pack a lot of clothes."

And I didn't. As soon as I got home I packed a bag and boasted about my readiness for adventure. My husband, Jean, and my youngest daughter Juliette kept quiet, as they have done through many of my personal announcements, because they know if they question me I won't be fit to live with. They are used to seeing me go through life intuitively, with inexplicable turns of events. They know it's torture for me, for example, to force myself to follow a recipe or to have to explain my plans for the day. I might throw figs in the stew, slide down the subway banister, or change my mind on the way to the public library and end up in a paddleboat on the canal. Why read *The Wind in the Willows* when you can *be* Ratty or Mole?

The new getaway suitcase was just another example of my need for the unexpected. But even I was surprised when the call that would activate the bag came within days. It was seven in the morning on a Saturday — a strange time for my phone to ring.

"Would you be at all interested," a writer colleague said, "in going on a vessel through the Northwest Passage?"

"The *Northwest Passage*?"

"Yes," said my friend Noah. "You might have heard that Russian icebreakers sometimes go up there and take passengers through. They like to have a writer on board, and I can't go, so I suggested you, but I wanted to check with you first that it might be something you'd like to do."

I thought of Franklin's bones, of the sails of British explorers in the colonial age, of a vast tundra only Inuit and the likes of Franklin and Amundsen and a few scientists had ever had the privilege of navigating. I thought of lead poisoning in the tinned food of Franklin's men, and of underwater graves and lost ships named *Erebus*, which meant "darkness," and *Terror*, which meant . . . I thought of my own British childhood, steeped in stories of sea travel. I thought of Edward Lear's Jumblies, who went to sea in a sieve. I thought of Queen Victoria and Jane Franklin, and of the longing and romance with which my father had decided to immigrate to Canada. I thought of all the books I'd read on polar exploration, on white men's and white women's attempts to travel the Canadian Far North.

I felt Noah was inviting me to go to the place where an imaginary world intersects with the real: a place where time flows differently from the linear way in which we have trained it to behave down here, in the southern world. The name "the Northwest Passage" is not written on world maps: it is an idea rather than a place. I'd long felt the power of that idea pull me in a way I couldn't fully understand.

My daughters were no longer helplessly small, and I'd already set off on a few modest travels, leaving them temporarily motherless. To look on a map at the route Noah had invited me to take thrilled me with images of ice, sea, and loneliness. For a writer, loneliness is magnetic. The very names on the map excited me: Lancaster Sound, Resolute, Gulf of Boothia. I knew that to go to these places would activate something inside me that had long lain dreaming.

I thought of the soul's journey to any kind of frontier, physical or spiritual. The Northwest Passage was the epitome, in my mind, of a place so exciting I'd never dared to imagine I might see it. How many times had I sat in my kitchen with my guitar, picking out the haunting melody of the old broadside ballad "Lady Franklin's Lament"?

In Baffin's Bay where the whale fish go
The fate of Franklin no man may know.
The fate of Franklin no man can tell.
Lord Franklin among his seamen do dwell . . .

"The ship," said Noah, "leaves this coming Saturday. "You'll be gone two weeks. I realize it's short notice . . ."

It was impossible for me to resist the vortex of excitement I felt that morning. Had the perfect response to this very invitation not been drilled into me only days before by Denise, on Aloise's dock? And when a man called Noah suggests you get on a ship, hadn't you better jump on board?

"My bags," I told him, "are already packed."

I TRIED TO remember what I'd put in the getaway bag Denise had prescribed: a little black dress, two pairs of underwear, a T-shirt, and a pair of jeans. I remembered reading that Franklin and his men had ventured to their deaths in masculine nineteenth-century versions of much this same idea: knickerbockers, silk shirts, stockings. I pictured the mummified remains of Franklin's men, which I'd seen in history books, with their preserved grimaces, their emaciated agony. I decided to call my friend Ross to ask him what he thought. I've known Ross since high school in Corner Brook, where at

seventeen we sat on dumpsters behind the main drag, looking up at the rock face looming behind Woolworths and pre-
tending we were in Naples. We had both ended up in Montreal,
which was, we decided, a pretty good substitute.

"The Northwest Passage?" said Ross.

"Yes. I'm a bit worried. Of course I'm excited, but . . ."

"I can understand that. I can understand you feeling a bit
worried."

"I mean Franklin's half-eaten body is still up there, under
the ice."

"Yes, but—"

"Cannibalized."

"I know, but you'll hardly—"

"And riddled with lead poisoning, and I know the ice is
melting up there, but it's still extremely off—outside of—
I mean, much of it is still uncharted, for goodness' sake."

"Yes, but surely the ship's crew will know what they're
doing. They wouldn't go up there if—"

"Right. But I mean you hear all the time, on the news . . ."

"I think you're understandably a little afraid. But I don't
think it's as . . ."

"You think I'll be all right? I mean Esther's twenty-one,
but Juliette is still only thirteen."

"Yeah, it's normal for you to worry about your daughters.
But that kind of worry can feel larger than, realistically—"

"You think I should just go?"

"Well, I mean, it's normal to wonder. But really, if you go,
what's the worst thing that can happen?"

This final question was one we would remember later.

But at the time, it seemed like a reasonable enough thing for him to ask, and the fact that he asked it assuaged my fears in the way that talking to an old friend can do even when there are no real answers. So I disobeyed Denise by repacking my bag, this time with a list in hand from the expedition leaders, whose packing instructions indicated I might need a woollen vest, and rubber boots, and hi-tech long johns unavailable to Franklin and his crew, whose delicates all had to be handstitched: the men vanished mere months before the invention of the sewing machine. I signed the expedition form and the waivers; I belonged to more modern times, a fact from which I derived a certain amount of courage. The forms and waivers came with photos of the other resource staff. I noticed they were nearly all men, and most had explorer-type beards. I happened to have a beard I'd crocheted out of brown wool on a train trip with my mother—it was a bit more Rasputin than Explorer, but it possessed loops that fit nicely around my ears, so I packed that as well.

The voyage list made no mention of musical instruments, but I'd read somewhere that Franklin's ship had carried some sort of piano and that the men had, before their deaths, tried to cheer each other in the typical English way by putting on pantomimes and singing and dancing for each other through the Arctic nights. I had been fooling around on an old German concertina for some time, and could play "Lady Franklin's Lament," a few Newfoundland songs, and "The Varsovienne," an old Warsaw folk dance that Gearóid Ó hAllmhuráin had taught me in St. John's. The concertina possessed no case, but I took it to Canadian Tire and fitted it in an insulated beer cooler that had a shoulder strap and claimed to be waterproof. If I grew lonesome in the Northwest Passage, or became stranded on an iceberg with all hope of rescue lost, I would have my concertina, which I remembered my father once said was also called a ship's piano.

"You should take my old Helly Hansen raincoat," my husband said as he saw me rolling up my flimsy rain gear and stuffing it in the bag. His coat was heavy-duty and looked like the tarp I used to fling over the woodpile.

"That'll never fit in the bag."

"Wear it."

"It has a hole under the arm."

"That is a perfect coat."

"And the pocket's ripped."

"Hang on." He went to the basement and came back with a brand new roll of duct tape, tore off a few strips, and plastered them artistically over the holes. "There you go. Now you're ready for the elements."

"You should take the rest of that roll of duct tape," Juliette piped up. She shoved it in the pocket now made mostly of its own self. And she was right. In the Northwest Passage, our ship and all its crew were going to need every scrap of duct tape we could lay our hands on.

chapter two

KANGERLUSSUAQ

WE WERE TO take a chartered plane from Toronto. At the airport our group straggled away from the well-dressed commuters with their streamlined cases on wheels: we lugged duffle bags and knapsacks with all manner of leather straps holding in binoculars, hiking sticks, and Audubon bird guides. The bearded men were out in full force; our self-named expedition leader and rear admiral were trying to figure out how to persuade airport officials that it was right and proper that they should be transporting guns.

"The guns are less for protection from wildlife," the gun-bearers shouted to the rest of us, "than they are to keep you lot in line if you get out of hand on the tundra."

Security officials wanted to separate me from my concertina, but they appeared not to know what to do with it. They sent me to Oversize Baggage, even though its case had been designed to hold no more than a dozen cans of beer.

"Where is this headed?" asked the person behind the X-ray machine.

"Greenland."

We were flying to Kangerlussuaq, where our ship would be waiting to take us on the first leg of the journey, up Greenland's southwest coast. Then we'd set off across Baffin Bay and head for Pond Inlet, the first Canadian stop. From there we'd sail up Eclipse Sound between the northwest tip of Baffin Island and Bylot Island to Lancaster Sound, gateway to Roald Amundsen's Northwest Passage. We were to traverse the passage and disembark in Kugluktuk, or "Coppermine," to board a chartered plane back to the south. Just thinking about that itinerary made my breath catch.

"Where is that?" The official behind the X-ray machine wore latex gloves. She had her hair in a ponytail. She did not know where Greenland was. She had my concertina in her hand, and was about to thrust it into a hole in the wall. Some people can regard that kind of circumstance with equanimity.

"Greenland," I said, with as much restraint as possible, "is the large, ice-covered land mass to the northeast of Canada."

If Greenland was unknown to airport security, how remote from the known universe was the rest of our voyage going to be?

On board the plane a kind of peace settled over the hundred or so passengers who would become fellow travellers. We no longer had to explain to anyone our rumpled and vaguely unsettling appearance — our expedition sacks, our trousers full of flaps and extra pockets. The passengers had begun to arrange themselves around the resource staff experts in their particular fields of interest. A group of birders huddled near ornithologist Richard Knapton, comparing camera lenses and matching up bird lists to see who longed to observe a white-tailed eagle, a red-throated loon, or a phalarope on our journey. I noticed a contingent of elegant Japanese voyagers travelling with a young woman who translated for them everything we were told by our pilot or our expedition leader. The rock people pored over a geology booklet the on-board geologist, Marc St-Onge, had prepared for us. Historian Ken McGoogan launched into his impassioned story of how Franklin had not discovered the Northwest Passage at all—it had really been an intrepid Scot named John Rae. Ken's wife, the artist Sheena Fraser McGoogan, had coloured pencils and sketchbooks ready to give to anyone who wanted to draw or record wonders we would see on the land. There was a shy, quiet anthropologist called Kenneth Lister, and a marine mammal biologist, Pierre Richard, who'd brought his elegant sister, Elisabeth, who had long wished to see the land he so loved. Many of these resource people had been in the Arctic before, but that didn't stop a nimbus of excitement from sizzling around their conversations as our plane took off.

"I've been here lots of times, on scientific projects," Pierre Richard told me. "But when you come for research it's not the same as coming on a voyage like this, where you have time to walk and think and indulge your pure love of the land."

A couple of seats down from me Nathan Rogers, our shipboard musician, laid his handmade guitar in a safe place, put a pair of noise-cancelling earphones on his shaved head, and sank into dreams of his own. Someone had told me that he was the son of Stan Rogers, the late Canadian folk icon whose haunting song, "The Northwest Passage" many of the passengers already knew by heart. I sat next to a Canadian Inuk woman, Bernadette Dean, who was, along with Greenlandic-Canadian Aaju Peter, a cultural ambassador; to them fell the task of teaching us about the North from the perspectives of Inuit women who have lived there all their lives — women who have come to know its animals, plants, and people, both indigenous and visiting, through long experience. As our plane took off, Bernadette busied herself writing in her notebook.

Our pilot had a cheerful American accent. As we flew over northern Quebec, he announced over the loudspeaker, "There you have it, folks, down below us... a whole lot of *nothing*."

There was a collective gasp, which the pilot possibly enjoyed.

"That's what he thinks," muttered Bernadette, looking up from her work. Corners of photographs stuck out from pages where she had made extensive notes. The jottings were interesting to me and she saw me glance at them. "I'm writing," she said, "to keep my mind off my little grandchild. He or she is going to be born, probably while we're on this expedition. I'm going to wish I was there. These are notes about my great-grandmother."

Her great-grandmother, Bernadette told me, was the Inuit clothing maker Shoofly, who in the early 1900s had fallen in love with a Boston whaling captain and given him many of her beadwork garments. He took them back to America, and Bernadette spent years trying to find them as part of her cultural heritage.

"I found them," she told me, "in storage, at the Museum of Natural History in New York City. It took me a long time to convince them to even let me come and see them. My own great-grandmother's clothes! Finally they gave me a window of two weeks. I accepted. I went down there and—here's a picture of me looking at the clothes." She showed me a photograph of herself lifting the garments from a museum drawer. "See, there's the Scandinavian curator." She pointed to a watchful figure standing beside her. "Look how close to me she is. See, they made me wear white gloves."

"That curator looks worried."

"They didn't want me to touch my great-grandmother's clothes. See her name? The whaling captain wrote her name, Shoofly, on her clothes."

"I see it."

"Then I said, 'That's not everything. That's not all the clothes. This set of garments has other parts. Where are they?' And that curator doubted me. She said there were no other parts. But I wanted to find them so I started looking. I started opening drawers until I found them. I found them and she didn't even know what they were. She had no idea. It felt like being a kid again, having a white teacher."

OUR PLANE TOUCHED down in Kangerlussuaq, where an old Russian bus waited, against sere grasses and rock faces seamed with snow, to take us to the ship. The landscape looked a bit like what I had seen of Labrador: rock loomed jagged and high against a big sky. Plants were dwarfed, yet sunlight shone through purple or white petals like a projector's light blazing through film and lighting up the vegetation in illumined detail.

As we piled onto the bus, Pierre Richard, the marine biologist, called to Nathan Rogers, "We have another musician on board—she has a concertina in her beer cooler!"

There are a lot of disparaging things real musicians have on the tips of their tongues about people with concertinas, and in this regard Nathan was no exception.

"Keep her miles from me, then," he said. "And hoist her concertina overboard—you gotta nip that kind of torture in the bud."

I knew Nathan's father, Stan, had died in a tragic plane mishap when Nathan was about four years old. On our voyage Nathan would sing his father's beloved song about the Northwest Passage, as well as songs from an extensive world-folk repertoire and compositions of his own. He would also teach the Inuit girls of Pond Inlet how to begin Mongolian throat-singing; but I knew none of this on the Russian bus. I just knew that with his shaven head, his radical tattoos and prickly comments, he looked like someone I might want to give a wide berth.

Our bus had rounded a corner in the crags of Kangerlus-suaq, and there in the bay was our ship, floating so crisp and blue and white it looked as if someone had ironed and starched it and stitched it into one of those three-dimensional pop-up picture books that had enchanted me when I was a child. When you open the pages, the world inside the book springs forward with hidden niches and bridges and stairs. Here, twinkling in the Greenland bay with its flags and decks and portholes, was a storybook ship I would come to love and care about as if it were a living being.

I'd spent years in Newfoundland, watching ships from the shore and wishing I was on them. In the distance they'd looked wistful, dreamlike—when their lights twinkled and they floated on the sea, distant and small, how mysterious they appeared, as if made not of substance but of thought and story. Now, as we boarded Zodiacs—motorized dinghies that waited on wet stones then sputtered into noise and spray as the helmsmen jolted us through the choppy water—our ship loomed larger, not a dream at all but muscled and humming from its own deep engine room.

As Noah had mentioned on the phone, the very first Arctic educational voyages had, like this one, been on Russian ice-breakers, but melting ice in the North meant that ships going through the Northwest Passage no longer needed to be utilitarian workhorses. Our ship was equipped for icy conditions, but it combined utility with grace. Its flags and decks were bright. On the main decks were several comfortably appointed areas whose simple lines satisfied everyone's appetite for ruggedness yet still bordered on elegance. In the forward lounge people could sit on expansive corner settees, or have a drink from the bar at small tables gathered around a stage area like a floating cabaret. At mid-ship we had another bar with couches and stools, and songbooks containing some smart person's best estimate of just about any song we might have wanted. In the dining room at the aft of the ship lay an airy, many-windowed expanse of white tablecloths and glittering stemware. There would be five-course menus that changed daily, as well as a buffet featuring endless slices of smoked Arctic char, yellow figs bobbing in their own syrup, capers and Danish cheeses, marinated peppers, olives, and piles of fresh provisions that Nordic suppliers would replenish in crates stacked on various beaches along our route until they could reach us no more.

"I feel," I confided to Elisabeth, who attracted me with her quiet, sympathetic air, "a bit like the Jumblies."

"The Jumblies?"

"Edward Lear's nonsense poem." The demented Englishman's poem had been a favourite of mine since I could read. "He wrote 'The Owl and the Pussycat,' too. He wrote limericks. But my favourite is 'The Jumblies.' He wrote it not long after the lost Franklin expedition: *Their heads are green, and their hands are blue, / And they went to sea in a Sieve*—a bit like Franklin, and their provisions were astonishing, like ours—*And forty bottles of Ring-Bo-Ree, / And no end of Stilton Cheese.*"

Elisabeth laughed. I sensed that her mind stretched into enigmatic places—I felt she had made herself a quiet sentinel, on guard for any ambush of curious news, and would remain calm in any circumstance. I liked this very much. She was slender and her hair floated in a cloud of curls that she tried to keep somewhat tame under a little beret. Next to her I was a bit of a clodhopping galoot, but I was used to that.

It was time to go downstairs to my cabin, number 108, and I realized on the narrow staircase that things below the main deck grew progressively less ornamental and plainer, more robust, in the descent. The air grew warmer, the passage walls more confining. The doors were small and some were made of metal, and the farther down I went, the louder came the thrum of industrial noise from the engine room. Higher up, through open doors, I had seen passengers' deluxe cabins with big windows looking out over Baffin Bay. By the time I descended to my own little cabin, there were tiny portholes, and when I pressed my nose to the glass, there lay the sea surface, at the level of my rib cage. I did not mind any of this: I found that the thrumming noise, with its accompanying vibrations, comforted me immensely. I was a small animal nestling ever closer to the heart of its mother, and we were setting off for the Northwest Passage — land of fables, channel of dreams.

chapter three

VIKING FUNERAL

I LOVED MY cabin. It was in the bowels of the ship next to
a door painted with the letters WTD — I would later find out
what that meant, and would be unsure whether to be comforted
or terrified by it. The cabin was tidy, with a sink and shower,
and lamps that let my cabin mate and me read and make notes
without disturbing each other's sleep. My cabin mate was the
young leader of the small Japanese expedition, and she worked
night and day as their translator. If we rose at six-thirty for an
early anchorage and expedition by Zodiac, Yoko got up before
six. If the northern lights put on a show that meant everyone
stayed up until midnight, she stayed up long past that, then
wrote expedition notes on her laptop for another hour. Everyone on the staff worked conscientiously like this, but she kept
some of the longest hours and displayed utter seriousness.

A lot of the time she was not in the cabin, which meant that,
as a reclusive writer, I had it gloriously to myself. I could lie on

my bunk and play my concertina, or kneel on the pillow and look out the porthole at the water mere inches from my face. I loved the fact that when I stood on the cabin floor, my body was below sea level. And when the ship moved, when we had broken anchor and were away, I gave in to that feeling of land-lessness beneath the body. While the ship tilted and the cabin hummed and shook with the engine, when the sea and clouds beyond our porthole started moving and the bit of Greenland we'd stood upon became a ribbon, then a fainter ribbon, then a line of dream-substance in the distance, I knew that being on a ship headed for Baffin Bay was a thing I'd longed for, unbeknownst to myself, all these years of hobbling on rock and boulder and valley. A Pisces, I was now in my marine ele-ment, and I wanted the journey to be endless.

There's a womb-like aspect to being in a cabin in a ship's belly, especially at night, when you are lying in the bunk before sleep comes. The cabin is so small that it would not be an acceptable size if it were on the ground, but because the ocean sways beneath, you feel an old feeling that might be the feeling of floating in amniotic fluid, and the walls can close in all they want: the ship is your mother, whose organs cradle you, and she is breathing. I wondered how I'd ever sleep on land again.

This floating away from the shore came not long after another, shorter sea voyage in which I'd begun to understand how the sea can wipe away the tumult of difficult times on land. Through the years of my first husband's illness, a malaise had entered me and nothing had been able to cure the root of it. I'd kept the small house where we'd lived with our daughter at the foot of a mountain called Butter Pot. The mountain often had a dusting of snow, the moon and stars illuminating its whiteness. A stream ran under our window and in summer, marsh toads and hermit thrushes gave the water music funny bass notes and sent mysterious bars of song — *"Carambola! Carondelet!"* — receding over the spruce and fir tops. The snipe in June made another sound: reaching great heights over the bog they would plummet, air winnowing through their tailfeathers with a phantom tone.

The snipe's call echoed the sadness of our life there, which, while beautiful in its simplicity, was spoiled by the fact that my husband was dying and our relationship had turned into one of many disappointments. In winter the pond behind our house froze and we skated in the moonlight: my last memories of our marriage are of James, in his overcoat and fur hat, walking on that ice, his daughter and I skating freely while he grappled with leaving all he loved, though much of it had departed from him before he died.

I walked miles behind that house. Songs came to me, and I sang them beside stones to which my daughter and I gave names, graceful stones that had personalities. On a boggy trail up the mountain I hunkered beside bog orchids, marvelling at the veins in their lobes, and I learned the names of plants like the blue-bead lily and the almond-scented twinflower, *Linnaea borealis*. I had not forgotten the visionary glimpse of reality I'd sensed in my youth, the feeling that the ordinary world, with its plants, stones, and people, became infused with a kind of glory that then retreated or hid. It had not come to me lately, and I'd begun to fear it had been a passing blessing of youth. When I was young I'd seen jaded people, bitter and disillusioned, and I'd vowed not to become like them. But it was hard, during poverty and illness, not to lose hope in that early intimation of glory, whatever it had been.

My disappointment made me hard to live with. I knew there were books that exhorted one to bloom where one was planted, to embrace the Zen of dying husbands and unwashed dishes and a well that froze in January and dried in August. But where was the book that would show me a map to the end of hardship? Whenever I could escape household duties I walked, ran, and wept in those trails in the woods, asking sky, alders, and water to talk to me, to bring me back that hint of something majestic and all-encompassing.

A pair of doves with blood-red drops on their necks cooed under our window. I kept a few hens, and wild partridges visited them at dusk, roosting in our birches. A boreal owl made his home in the black spruce across the stream, and there were loons. The marsh hid a family of ducks that local hunters kept trying to find; each spring there were new ducklings. I listened to all the birds, and to the wind, and I suppose they were talking to me, but at the time I did not feel spoken to. I beseeched whatever life was in that outdoor world, whatever Great Spirit might reside there, to teach me something, anything at all, any scrap of wisdom, or insight, or comfort. I sensed secrets ebbing and receding, and begged them to show themselves. But I was clamouring on the edge of a silent and unyielding bell.

It frustrated me that life had become much harder: that motherhood, poverty, and illness meant I no longer had energy or vision to ask any question larger than whether or not my hens had laid eggs for dinner, whether I could thaw the pipes leading from the well, or how long it would take for my green firewood to give heat instead of smoke that permeated the kitchen and made it impossible for us to stop coughing. I had a guitar and a couple of notebooks filled with lyrics, and if there was one song that epitomized how I felt then, between visits to food banks and the hospital, it was Stephen Foster's "Hard Times":

> 'Tis the song, the sigh of the weary,
> Hard times, hard times, come again no more
> Many days you have lingered around my cabin door;
> Hard times, come again no more.

Someone had given our name to agencies that gave out Christmas hampers, and we were given three turkeys, but had nothing to eat with them. When I tell my second husband about the turkeys, he says, "Why didn't you trade two of those turkeys with someone else, for some vegetables and bread and cake?" which seems like a sensible idea. But we cooked and ate the three turkeys, and when the last one was gone, we received a supper invitation from a Samaritan who did not know us well, but who must have known there was a dying man in the house and must have guessed we were hungry. She lived alone and was still working on the remains of her own turkey. She served us turkey soup, and I suppose she still thinks my tears on her tablecloth were tears of gratitude.

When James died, a pall lingered. I had loved the little house we'd called our gypsy caravan, but it contained shadows from which I needed to free myself. This took time and involved shedding objects that had accumulated in hidden corners. One corner in the basement held many pieces of sadness: papers and paintings and mementos connected with James, along with special clothes he had loved. Anything I'd thought important to save for his daughter or his closest friends and family, I had saved and given. But there remained boxes and chests that contained dark and powerful memories, and before I could leave that house I had to do something with them.

"What you need," said Christine, my brother Michael's *conjointe*, as they say in Montreal, "is a Viking funeral."

"A what?"

"You gather the things, you bring them to me out in Western Bay. We build a raft for it all and get our dory and tow the raft out in the bay and set fire to it. I'll row you out."

There was something so final and beautiful about this. I said yes.

At sunset I showed the last few things to Christine and to the little procession that had formed to see everything float and burn.

"What about this? It's his wolf-fur hat."

"Burn it."

"And this? A copy of the *Declaration of Independence* on parchment that he made when he was into calligraphy."

"That'll flare up nicely."

"What about his medieval waistcoat?"

"Throw it on the heap."

Christine was a perfect boatman. In her pocket she had a

mickey of vodka she'd chilled in the freezer, and every few minutes she handed it to me and I took a deep ceremonial swig. There was no doubt in her form or in her bearing about what we were doing. She looked as if she had been the boatman for hundreds of Viking funerals. The onlookers, too, looked as if they had attended this sort of occasion for millennia — especially the children, who did cartwheels over the wild grasses which grew brighter and brighter green under the reddening sky. By the time we'd hauled the raft down to the beach, the sky was mauve and stars had come out. Christine had a bottle of lighter fluid in another pocket. She poured a hefty dose over James's possessions, then we climbed in the dory and the crowd pushed us out into the water.

It felt great to float. I had total faith in Christine, in her ability to permeate James's things with flame accelerant, in her taste in vodka, and in her oarsmanship. Now it was just the two of us, and the brooding sky, and the lovely, lapping, undulating salt water. I had never felt the rightness of any destructive activity as strongly as I felt the rightness of this one. In the dark we could still see our friends on the beach — small now, as we were far out in the bay.

"I want you to think about everything you want for the future," Christine said. "And I want you to think about how thoroughly you're letting these things from the past go. How great that is, and how it will free you."

Her oars swished and dripped and I loved that sound, and I loved what she said. She has long, brown hair and light from somewhere lit parts of it, and she is tall and strong. I felt I was in the hands of someone who knew what she was doing, even if only for the duration of this operation.

"Okay," I said.

"I'm going to soak the things in some more lighter fluid," she said, "and here are the matches. When you're ready, light the pile."

She gave me the matches and I lit one and held it to some of the papers. They weren't James's diaries — I'd saved those for his daughter — and they weren't our old love letters, which I still have in a black bag. But he'd kept carbon copies of radio plays he'd written, and copies of his newspaper articles about art, and research materials on the Shroud of Turin and Richard Brothers and the British Israelites and liner notes from vintage Gregorian chants and other things like that which depressed me and drove me a bit nuts and which I never wanted to see again as long as I lived. I lit the papers.

"Light the medieval shirt. Light the wolf hat."

I lit half a dozen matches and nestled their flames among the floating materials, and at first I thought none of it would catch. But a flame caught and then came a blaze that we knew would grow and not fizzle out. Christine took out a pair of scissors I had not known about, and she cut the string that connected the raft to our boat, and she rowed us farther out into the bay so we could look at the blaze. It burned and floated on top of the dark water, and we heard a commotion from the little gathering on the beach far away as they watched it too. There was something alchemical and primal and magical about seeing such a big fire floating on the sea, and knowing what it contained. There was always the thought, coming from some corner of life or of death or of the basement where the burning

things had so long lain, that we shouldn't be doing this. But
stronger than that thought came the feeling that it was right;
it was liberating. As the blaze continued to burn, Christine
rowed, slowly, in a widening circle around the flames, asking
if I wanted to stay at this vantage point or keep moving, and
obeying every time I asked her to hold still or row some more.
Every now and then we'd stop in the ocean, and she would
make an S curve with her oar so that we could stay in one spot,
and I could feel the satisfaction of watching the destruction of
everything that had tried to trap and hold me to sad or difficult
memories. The trappings were all going up in flames, and the
ocean was going to swallow them.

I don't know how Christine knew how to conduct the timing of it all, but at some point while the fire was still going,
but was perhaps diminishing, she asked if it was okay with me
that we slowly return to shore. I said it was, and she rowed so
I could continue to watch the flames, and she somehow timed
it so that the very last flame was burning small and lonely as
I heard the pebbles of the shoreline schmizzle under our dory,
and I felt the love and support and comfort of our shore companions, who were silent now, as we all watched that last
flame. And as that flame died, what should Christine and her
Viking funeral somehow bring to pass, but from the eastern
edge of the sky to the western hem, a slow-burning, blazing-
white shooting star.

Now the rocking of our ship gave me that feeling, again,
of land troubles falling away, dissolving. There is no line or
corner in a wave, no way for cares of the world to hook or snag
you. Floating up the southwest coast of Greenland toward the

villages of Sisimiut, Ilulissat, and Upernavik was an extension of that healing journey in Christine's little Viking boat, unmoored and heading for the unknown.

chapter four

SISIMIUT

IN SOUTHWEST GREENLAND the land reminded me of New-foundland, yet we were far enough north that the similar-ities had limits. Greenland's fireweed is *Chamerion latifolium*, a dwarf cousin of the lupin-shaped plumes that signal late summer in Newfoundland and the rest of southern Can-ada; it struck me as brave and diminutive, somehow insistent despite its size. It called your eye to itself and said, "Be hon-est and clean-cut, no need to shout or loom large, or be in any way extravagant"—perhaps an apt message for Greenland's national flower.

The Danish influence gives southern Greenland a bright, neat appearance: there's an atmosphere of crisp freshness and industry. Houses sit neatly on rocky hills, painted in loud primary colours that shout cheer along with the daisies' and fireweed's yellow and purple. There's a European modern-ity, imposed on an ancient land whose dwellers go back 4,500

years to people of the Saqqaq, Dorset, and Thule cultures—
who share ancestry with Canada's Inuit and whose diet traditionally consisted of fish, birds, whale, seal, and reindeer. I
was familiar with the American writer Gretel Ehrlich's stunning book *This Cold Heaven*, in which she chronicles seven
seasons travelling in Greenland by dogsled and kayak, with
local hunters and descendants of the famed Danish-Inuit
explorer Knud Rasmussen. Greenland's north, according to
Ehrlich, remains a place of ancient ways, imperilled but mostly
intact—but here in the southern part, old hunters have begun
to trade a life of precarious freedom and hardship for work in
the Danish fishery, and it is now not uncommon for people to
pay a high price for a Danish chicken rather than eat wild auk
or seal.

Our first stop, Sisimiut, might have been 75 kilometres
north of the Arctic Circle, but the currency was Danish kro-
ner. I visited shops and saw aisles of the same cheese graters,
plastic hair clips, pink wafer biscuits, and packets of licorice
I'd seen in suburban European and North American dis-
count shops. There were shiny packets of Danish cookies and
all manner of European goods. Like the houses, boats, and
picket fences around the local graveyard, everything in the
Danish shop aisles was tidy and groomed, as if someone kept
watch over the whole set-up to ensure it did not depart from
a northern European sense of order. Yet underlying Sisimiut's
imposed Danish brightness lingered something indestructible
and indigenous to the Arctic.

It reminded me of the islands of St-Pierre and Miquelon
off the southern Newfoundland coast: owned by France and

kept as a symbolic remnant of colonial proprietorship, their rock and shore know cod and wild horses, rum and puffin and tern. They know bleak grey tides and summers not even the dreamiest French impressionist could render dappled or soft. Yet the shops sell French produce: wine, slender green beans, French butter, and baguettes. The schools have French classrooms whose students are taught the French history children learn in Paris. While there is scarcely enough road to take a Sunday drive, the residents possess Citroens, Renaults, and Peugeots. In St-Pierre and Miquelon this tension — between the old geography of rock jutting out of the north Atlantic and the imposed culture of France — creates a forlorn atmosphere, as if the towns are in a time capsule; child-towns orphaned by a mother country who claims them for bureaucratic reasons. There persists a feeling that the place lies forgotten when it comes to love.

Greenland has a different understory. The Danish influence feels closer, more current and immediate — but it also feels like a layer superimposed on that long-standing other culture, where people survive by clinging to an old connection with the animal world. Underpinning that connection, and making it possible, is the fact that in Greenland, unlike in northern Canada, people have held on to their working dogs.

Indeed, the first thing I noticed after the layer of Danish influence was the dogs. In the villages of southwestern Greenland, every shed has colourful ropes and dog harnesses hanging from hooks and nails. As I took to the lanes and paths, Greenlandic huskies watched me from their posts on tussocks and stones with their dark, intelligent eyes. On the paths, I encountered more dogs than people, and I realized that the human population of these little towns — Ilulissat is home to 4,000 — is tiny compared to the number of dogs.

I had a sort of enchanted status on the ship, since I was hired to be a resident writer; but I'd been engaged at the last minute, so my status was unofficial. I didn't have teaching duties like other resource staff — passengers began breaking off to form coteries around their experts of choice. Marc St-Onge explained the glacial fjords. Filmmaker John Houston told us how to relate to people on the land and screened his new film, *The White Archer*, a drama based on a story in his father James Houston's 1967 collection of Inuit legends.

"Be brave," Houston told passengers. "Give when you're out in the community. If you're speaking through a translator, look into the person, not at the translator."

On deck I told him I'd written a novel, *Annabel*, about a dual-gendered person.

"A person like that," he said, "has a shamanic nature. Inuit pronouns have no gender. You don't say here *he* comes, here *she* comes. You say *here come those two*. You have to listen to the shamanic world, and to dreams."

I listened carefully. I wanted to learn as much as any other passenger did. On the land I relied on my solitude, my walking and observations, but I also gravitated toward Bernadette Dean and Aaju Peter because I wanted their Inuit and Greenlandic perspectives — I wanted to hear what women of this land had to say, and was less interested in the old European male Arctic explorer stories to which the history buffs thrilled. I wanted to listen to the passengers as well, not to teach them but to learn from them, and I could do this by speeding up or slowing down on the paths, falling in with Gillian from England or Penny from Texas or world-wandering Gerald, who appeared to have no homeland apart from his battered shoes and his walking stick. I loved listening to their stories. I learned many had come to the Northwest Passage for healing. More than one woman had lost her life's companion in the preceding year, and there'd been other losses, yearnings, personal tragedies, and transformations that had led people to this ship.

Nothing was solid. Paradox lay everywhere. Jean, whose husband had longed to make this journey but had died before they could embark, possessed great inner joy. Another woman, deep in pain over the recent loss of her life's partner, was still somehow able to relieve others of physical sprains and aches by laying her healing hands on their injuries. I tended to follow and listen to the wandering souls, rather than those who knew the most facts about the land we were exploring.

But I also liked being alone. I picked my way up and down Sisimiut's steep hills toward the whitewashed crosses of the graveyard, trying to stay apart, speaking only when spoken to, wanting the silent, unbroken gaze between myself and the town's sled dogs to be the only communication. But it appeared I had a talkative companion.

"Crosses like the ones on those graves," Nathan Rogers said, "are pre-Christian."

"They are?"

I remembered hearing my mother, deep in her Jehovah's Witness booklets, mutter about pagan crosses. But Nathan was harder to ignore. Like everything under the Greenland sun, he shone as if laundered, and he had such a genuine smile and such wild tattoos I almost forgot how he'd insulted my poor concertina.

"They signify the swords of fallen soldiers."

"How do you know?"

"A degree in comparative religion sort of helps." He proceeded to bring me up to date on the roots of Freemasonry and Mormonism.

"I had a friend," I told him, "who let her basement apartment out to a couple of Mormons. She used to give them a raisin bun and tea every evening and they'd preach to her. Something about tablets of gold in the American woods, blazing with truth for the New World."

"That's right. Joseph Smith."

"Anyway, they converted her. She became a Mormon missionary in Bucharest. But there's something I'm dying to know."

"What's that?"

I hesitated. We had navigated higgledy-piggledy lanes. A church bell rang. Noon. A husky in the cove raised its snout and howled, a long, lonesome sound that twined and coiled and floated through the whitewashed crosses. We could no longer see the ship, or the main road, or the other passengers. I suddenly became afraid.

"Would we hear the ship's horn if it blew?" The horn signified we were to get back on board and leave Sisimiut behind.

"Maybe. Is that the thing you were dying to know?"

"No. What I wanted to know is, what about the man, the

naked man in the Bible, who — just as the disciples have fallen asleep and Judas is about to betray Jesus with a kiss — runs inexplicably through the Garden of Gethsemane? Nobody ever talks about him." It was a question I asked anyone who professed to know anything about religion. Nobody had ever answered it; they hadn't even tried. Not my mother; not my husband's uncle, the *Père blanc* African missionary; and not my first husband, who had professed to know the New Testament better than he knew the Conception Bay Highway bus schedule. Those people all took one glance at that question and changed the subject.

"The naked man," Nathan said, "was fulfilling a rite of a Dionysian cult."

"He was?"

"It has to do with the Eastern Star. It has to do with mysteries hidden in plain view." By the time Nathan elaborated we were at the summit of a tussock beyond which I saw that our ship was much farther away than I'd hoped.

"I wonder if I turned my tag," I said.

Passengers leaving the ship each had a two-sided tag hanging on a hook and marked with their cabin number: green meant you were safely back on the ship, red meant you were not on board. If you'd forgotten to turn your tag to red as you left the ship, which was easy to forget at first, it appeared to all hands as if you might be having a nap in your cabin. It crossed my mind that this might afford an excellent way to get rid of a tiresome husband. But I knew, too, that the tags were not a game.

"Did you hear the story that some of the passengers were

telling about a lost couple?" I asked Nathan. "They wandered too far on a coral reef during a southern expedition on another ship. Hours after that ship departed the reef, long after tides had washed the pair asunder, someone noticed they weren't in the dining room."

"Are you afraid that might happen to us?"

"I wouldn't want to get left behind."

"That won't happen to us. Come on, we'll get you back to the ship." He started back down the confusing lanes and I realized he was very serious about reassuring me. "My father," he explained, "died lifting passengers to safety."

"On that Air Canada plane."

"Flight 797. On June 2, 1983."

"I know. He got stuck in the plane. I'm really sorry. You were what, only three or four years old?"

"He wasn't stuck in the plane. He was at the exit, calling to passengers who couldn't see for the smoke, telling them the way out, carrying them, throwing them to safety. If ever we have an accident on this ship, or anywhere, that's the way I want to go. So don't worry, we aren't lost and you aren't going to get left behind."

We managed to hurry around a maze of little streets down-hill and shoreward in time to duck into the village artists' workshop before the last horn. Aaju Peter held the foot of an Arctic ptarmigan set in a chain. It was white, its feathers fluffy as fur, and Aaju looked at every part of it with tenderness.

"It was made in the town where I was born," she said, "by a southern white woman. I have to buy it. Art has no colour."

I felt something open inside me. I might have expected an

Inuk woman to lay that ptarmigan foot down as soon as she realized a white woman had made it. In accepting the white artist's work, Aaju made me feel that I, too, had a right to find my own truth on this voyage. Yes, I was a descendant of colonial Englishmen, and no, no one in my family had been born Canadian: in fact, I felt like a cultural orphan. But if Aaju was right, if art had no colour, maybe my perception, the raw material for my writing, also deserved to be treated by me with tenderness rather than self-doubt.

LATER, ON BOARD the ship, Nathan performed "The Northwest Passage." His guitar was a beautiful, hand-made instrument, and to perform, Nathan had brought along stunning shirts embellished with magnificent Western and Celtic designs. His whole public persona took on a true musician's extra wattage, and he introduced the song knowing full well how deeply it had settled into people's ideas of what made this whole journey important. I wondered how it felt to share his father's music when he had not had the chance to know Stan Rogers through any manner other than that of the lifeline of his songs. Singing them must have felt like both a public and a very private act, and I think many sons of lost, heroic fathers would never have been able to do it.

"I can't begin to tell you," Nathan told everyone, "how cool it is to be doing this trip with you folks. It's one thing to finish your own business: another thing to finish someone else's." And then he began singing his father's song.

Throughout the voyage Nathan would sing in many

voices: his father's voice came through him, and that took a certain kind of strength that made him a conduit. But he has his own voice as well, which is a more modern voice, more complex and nuanced and imbued with Nathan's own esoteric psychology. It is strangely psychic and muscular at the same time, and always linking ancient and future worlds.

As night fell, in a shipboard ceremony to welcome us to the North, Aaju held the body of a red-throated loon, hollowed and filled with tinder-dry lichen.

"It's very flammable," Aaju said, coaxing a piece of lichen out of the loon. She lit a spark with flint stones and used a stick to carry the flame to the lichen fragment. She then transferred flame from the lichen to a traditional stone lamp whose wick, she told us, had been twisted out of willow cotton and seal fat.

"Sometimes," she said, "we use whale or caribou fat." She was drinking coffee out of a Starbucks travel mug. "The lamp, when it is lit, can melt snow for a whole pot of water." I noticed then that the traditional Inuit patterns tattooed on each of Aaju's hands imitated the flames of the stone lamp she was holding. She bears tattoos on her forehead, as well; many Inuit women, I've learned, are reintroducing these body markings after generations of cultural suppression.

Next, Bernadette told us about Aaju's clothing.

"*Tuilli*," she explained, referring to Aaju's anorak, or inner parka, "means 'most practical garment.' See how it's designed with a V on its back? That's to signify the beak of a ptarmigan. It shows respect for that bird. The pointed hood means the caribou's tongue, and the shape of each of Aaju's boots resembles the head of a seal because the seal gives us fat for the lamp, and it gives its skin to keep our feet, hands, and bodies warm."

All electric lights were out in the lounge where the ceremony took place, and the seal-oil lamp gave off a glow that did not blare or rise beyond a gentle light, yet somehow lit every attentive face in the room. The flame burned along the wick of twisted tundra plants like a line of glowing fluid. Aaju cut raw seal heart with her ulu's curved blade and shared it. I ate a piece, sweet and cold, dense and bloody. Beyond the orange light I saw the blue Arctic night press against the windows. I moved out into it.

Many of the other passengers had gone to bed early, but a few lingered outside in a blue glow I'd seen nowhere else. The deck was a marginal zone between the womb of one's cabin and the wild North that now lay around us. It was not full of the coffee pots and biscuits or the music and comfort of the forward lounge and other communal parts of the ship where there was social discourse. On the deck people left you alone, or you held chance encounters with other wandering souls, and you soaked in the strange midnight gleam.

After the lamplighting ceremony I found Nathan and Bernadette outside in the shadows. I think sometimes performers and teachers need to recharge after they have given of themselves and shared publicly things that are actually personal and very private. The three of us stood watching the ship create a lit-up wake behind us as we sailed north out of Sisimiut.

"With respect to Aaju and the others," Bernadette told me softly, "the lamplighting ceremony is supposed to happen in winter, not this time of year."

This reminded me of times in Newfoundland when I had

heard Chris Brookes of the Mummers Troupe say that the mummers' ritual play — an ancient and powerful mystery connected with fertility, magic, and the solstice — should not be performed at any time other than the twelve days of Christmas: any other performance of it diluted its power. There would be many times on this voyage when such conflicts would come into play. There is just no way so many layers of cultural importance can intersect without these kinds of discussions. Bernadette's own story imbued her with intensity and loveliness, and with pain as well. I loved her tension, her unwillingness to fabricate a seamless and perfect story, and her insistence that we needed to respect the land to a degree none of us yet understood.

"The environment is boss," Bernadette said. "Water, land, wind, sky — these are the only ones with absolute freedom."

She was still, she told me, grappling with the idea of forgiveness for the profound hurt done to her people by my people. "That's why I'm on this boat," she said. "To turn my anger into something good."

IN THE ARCTIC night a kind of seafarer's forgiveness prevailed. It helped me connect with the others and overcome some of my introverted inclinations. The shadows hid me mercifully, yet contained enough light to help me see others' faces and read ambiguity there. The more Aaju and Bernadette taught me, the more dignity and compassion I felt toward myself. The more Nathan shared through his songs, the more like a song I felt my own life, all our lives, become. Standing on deck with the others I felt invited to the human party in a way I had perhaps not felt before — paradoxically more grounded as our ship floated away from any ground I'd known.

I had begun to learn about the beauty of the passengers — how a northern voyage bonds people and makes us suspend usual judgments. Landlubbers have more space than sailors do, and give each other a wider berth so as not to have to deal with each other's inconvenient traits. But on a ship there is no way to throw personality overboard; each passenger trails a big balloon containing all the idiosyncrasies he or she manages to hide on dry land. Maybe land is porous enough to absorb these traits and make them invisible. On the ship there was nowhere for them to hide; yet, suddenly, they became endearing. At night in my bunk I thought of the mysteries underlying people's personalities, both those I'd met on the ship and those I'd left at home. I thought of my father, and of how many things about his own move from the Old to the New World had been private and hardly understood by his children.

Generational patterns recur, and my ancestors have always moved between urban and wild landscapes. When my father was a kid in the Second World War, in Jarrow in the north of England, his teacher gave the kids a bean each, in a jam jar with wet tissue paper. The sight of his bean sprouting in the jar made my dad run home and ask his mother if she had anything he could plant in soil on top of the air raid shelter.

"I've just been peeling a few carrots," my grandma said. "Here, plant these."

"She gave me the carrot tops," he told me. "There wasn't much soil on top of the air raid shelter. In fact there wasn't any.

I carried it from wherever I could find it in a toy bucket. But the carrot tops grew and I never looked back."

I'd been to Newfoundland for a visit and he was driving me back to Deer Lake Airport on his way to his log cabin, where he needed to harvest his beets. It had finally occurred to me, in my late forties, to ask him how he had learned to be such a great gardener.

My dad is self-sufficient in leeks, Brussels sprouts, beets, string and broad beans, strawberries, and potatoes. He takes snow peas to the local Chinese restaurant in Corner Brook where, in return, they treat him kindly with his Saturday night takeout orders all year round. He used to win trophies before we immigrated to Canada, in the leek shows at the Methodist church behind our house on Hainingwood Terrace in Bill Quay. One of the first things he did when we arrived in Newfoundland was acquire enough crown land to grow every vegetable our family would ever eat. Over several summers, as he built his cabin, he cleared acres out of which we hauled boulders and roots to make his cabbage grounds. We also peeled the logs for the cabin, using tools he made based on a log-peeling blade he ordered from the Lee Valley catalogue. "A good workman," he said, "makes his own tools."

"What was the main reason we came to Canada?" I asked him in the car. I knew he'd left Les Lakey and Joe Cramm behind, friends with whom he'd bred goats and hitchhiked to Coldstream and sung in pubs, and I knew my mother hadn't known how hard it would be to watch her father grow old and blind and ill and then die from across the ocean. I knew my dad was happy to have left England and he always said he had no regrets, but I wanted to hear him tell me why he'd left everything familiar.

"Freedom," he said, as if any fool knew that. "Every stick in England was owned and accounted for, and still is."

You find out things about your parents when they wish you to do so, or as you gain perspective, or as they tell stories to your kids that they never got around to telling you. My dad told Esther, my daughter, how he saw the Beatles at the Cavern Club before they were famous. He told my daughter Juliette that as a boy he longed to be a mechanic but on the day of his apprenticeship the master mechanic found out he was forbidden to take a student because he had no toilet on the premises, so my dad became a plumber at the shipyard instead. Later he became a woodworker, designing mahogany sideboards and tables as well as refinishing and making replicas of Queen Anne and other period desks, chairs, and divans. He taught woodworking for years, then had his own furniture business for a long time after that.

"How did you learn to make furniture, Dad?"

Again, that look—how could a child of his be so obtuse? "I learned it from books."

"But books, Dad—I can't learn anything three-dimensional from books. Someone has to show me."

"Well, I learned a lot of what I know from books."

I remembered piles of books on the coffee table he'd made, and on the bookshelf he'd built: books on refinishing wood, on joinery and upholstery, as well as on mysteries of the Mayan pyramids and on polar exploration. A Punjabi doctor had entrusted him once with refinishing a divan of carved ebony, an ancient piece transported from Kashmir, and he studied how to do it and then he went ahead.

"If you have a visitor," he told me when I was small and he was buttering me some toast, "and you give that visitor bread and butter, make sure you butter the bread right to the very edges."

With pieces of walnut left over from the legs of a chair, he carved Adam and Eve. He made a cat ready to pounce, copper vases, enamelled dishes, and a kaleidoscope of glass and mirrors with purple, gold, and green starbursts of crumpled Quality Street toffee papers. He taught me how to hammer and cut scrap copper pipe and powder it with enamel designs and fire it in a kiln to make necklaces, and offered to teach my daughter to do it too. He taught me how to make hooked rugs out of coffee sacks and rag strips and a hook made from a filed nail hammered into the handle of an old rolling pin. But one thing he made was different from all these other things, and I wondered about it for a long time, and I still do.

I was in junior high school at the time; he was still in his thirties. All of a sudden he took to sitting in his leather rocker with a board and a tray of grey, tan, green, and blue paints in plastic vials, working on a paint-by-number painting of men in a sailboat. I remember the myriad blue outlines he had to daub with a tiny brush, each with a blue number printed inside. It was a solitary effort that went on for weeks, maybe months. He didn't mind my watching him so it became a quiet ritual: I'd kneel on the carpet watching the boat, the sails, and the ocean waves emerge out of seemingly unconnected scraps of colour: here was light, here was shade. The rest of the

household continued normally around this calm, oceanic centre — my mother rolling pastry beyond the hatch in the dining
room, through which we could see one square of the kitchen;
my brothers beating each other to a pulp and watching *Get
Smart,* or playing Risk and G.I. Joe. I can smell the linseed oil
now. How monochromatic the colour choices seemed to me —
where were red and purple? How could anything transform
into a scene with those limited hues? Yet it did, and the painting went on the wall above my mother's sewing machine table,
where it still hangs.

I wondered about the painting because it didn't fit in with
all the other things my dad designed or made from scratch.
What had made him devote so much time, his most precious
resource, to doing something that, to my mind, seemed little more creative than a jigsaw puzzle? I'd forgotten, with the
teenage superiority my daughter now exhibits so exquisitely
toward me, that when my dad made this painting of men braving the sea, he'd already left everything he knew behind in the
Old World. Only a few years prior to working on the painting
he'd voyaged to a new-found land which to his British friends,
his mother and perhaps his father, and anyone he'd ever
known, represented the ultimate in wilderness and unknown
possibility. His mother had said to me before our family left
England, "When you get to that place, watch out for bright
green grass. It isn't grass, it's bog, and if you walk on it, it can
swallow you."

"Freedom," my dad told me, was what he sought in Canada; and what exemplified freedom more than sails in the wind
on an open sea? I found out, with time, that his painting wasn't

some random image sold in Woolworths near the jigsaw puzzles and Phentex yarn. The image was based on one of the most famous American paintings in existence, the Winslow Homer piece originally called *A Fair Wind*, first shown in 1876 at America's centennial exhibition and renamed *Breezing Up* by critics and a public who saw in it the New World's dream of boundless invention and discovery.

"Yes," my mother said, when I asked her about our emigration. "It was exciting, the New World and all that. But maybe we didn't realize, about you, the children, we were removing you from your roots." Yes — hadn't I left Rhona and Deborah to play elastic skipping without me on Hainingwood Terrace? Hadn't the Newfoundland kids dragged me behind the school at recess and taught me how to lose my Geordie accent and speak like a Newfoundlander?

In my twenties I'd lived in a fishing outport, in search of surrogate grandparents among the old fishermen and their wives who still made jam and told old-time stories over the turnip-garden fences. The first greeting from any such acquaintance was, "Where do you belong?" No xenophobic unfriendliness, this was an age-old greeting that really meant, "From where have you come, kind stranger?" But when you've left a country behind as a child, you don't know where you belong. You constantly try to put down roots but they won't hold the way they would have had your father done as generations of his people had, and stayed where he was born. You remain in a state of slight yet constant unbelonging, a rootless unease that can remain incurable in the new land unless something happens to change everything.

Maybe my father re-painted Winslow Homer's image so he could learn how to make an oil painting: how does one transpose a three-dimensional scene onto a board? How do you create chiaroscuro and depth of field? Was he experimenting as he had done while teaching himself to make desks, cabinets, and enamelled copper pieces? Or was the painting's New World spirit of discovery the lure that attracted him?

I've never asked him. But I know that in 1876, while *A Fair Wind* hung at the first official World's Fair, the steamer *Pandora* sailed from Southampton in its second search for the lost Franklin expedition. Jane Franklin had died eleven months before, after funding seven previous searches. But her death did not end the search expeditions, which continued beyond that first World's Fair, through the nineteenth and twentieth centuries, and into my own twenty-first century journey through the Northwest Passage, imbuing it with an excitement every passenger on our ship sensed. Franklin and his ships had never been found: they accompanied us in the Arctic night, perhaps closer than many of us dared think.

Between Franklin's 1845 disappearance and the 1876 World's Fair in which ten million visitors came to the grounds where Homer's painting was displayed, the European soul remained gripped by the notion of a northwest passage to the Indies. Only a hundred years before, when the partly-literate Samuel Hearne embarked in 1769 on his own journey to describe the area from Hudson's Bay to what Britain then called the Northern Ocean, Britain itself had never been accurately mapped: that nation's Ordnance Survey department did not exist until 1791. Even to this day, Canadian Coast

Guard surveyors continue to explore the Arctic by ship, on foot, and by sonar submarine robot, attempting to complete navigational charts that have remained as fluid as the waters over Franklin's bones. Our own expedition leaders gave us each a map on which to track our voyage, and it wasn't long before one of the more learned passengers observed that this New Century Map of Canada, made by the Royal Canadian Geographical Society and the National Atlas of Canada, contained an error of several degrees. It would later be revealed that even our captain's navigational charts did not tell the complete truth about what lay ahead of us, since much of the Arctic remains uncharted and the land, wind, and ocean themselves are forever in flux.

What my father wanted from Newfoundland was what Americans yearned for when they viewed Homer's sailors at that first World's Fair. It's what passengers on my own ship craved, the thing we've all sought through the ages. My father might have called it freedom. I didn't know what to call it, there in our first Greenland anchorage at Sisimiut, other than a glimmering, a beckoning; something in the ice, something promising in the Arctic light.

"We lost your roots," my mother said. "For freedom," my father insisted. On our ship, roots no longer held the key to life: here, wind and water rocked me. Floating at anchor outside Sisimiut I felt a reprieve from my parents' conflict, from the tyranny of lines and borders, and even from the tension between freedom and belonging within myself.

chapter five

CATHEDRALS OF ICE

WE BEGAN MOVING up the coast, away from Sisimiut's fjords, which remain ice-free all year round and give Greenland the green part of its name. I was impatient to go farther north — I wanted to see why Greenland is known as "the mother of ice." In Newfoundland I'd sat on a cliff on the Avalon Peninsula, watching the moon light masses of ice that had floated from the coasts of Greenland and Labrador; now we were headed for the calving ground of every iceberg Newfoundland and Labrador had ever seen. I was burning to go beyond this shore where things looked so familiar: the mist, fishing boats, the rocky outcrops sewn with acid-loving sorrels and fireweed, and the brightly painted houses. I wanted to leave the Danish influence that had imposed its cultural layer on an ancient Inuit society, and to see what only the most rare and fortunate Europeans had seen — the higher Arctic zone, where surely colonial influence must be forced to give way to the elements.

A sense of adventure intensified on the ship. I felt it among the passengers, many of whom were much older than I was. We'd come to see the last great wilderness before it melted and before humans sprinted to the finish line in our collective race to homogenize the planet. Everyone on board wanted an adventure and now inhaled the palpable thrill the Far North blows into anyone who has longed for it. All the scientists on board were excited, though they'd experienced similar terrain. Even those who had travelled before with our ship had never made this precise journey. We were planning, in the words of the shipboard historian, to essentially follow Roald Amundsen's first successful route through the Northwest Passage, but anything could happen: weather or ice could intervene, and the ship might be forced to change its planned course at any time.

As we inched toward the ice I felt a duality pervade life on the ship: a tension between comfort and peril. Two lovely urns stood in the forward lounge, ready to dispense ice water and cold orange juice. A bread chef baked mountains of sweet rolls daily, and to spread on them there was Danish butter made with cultured cream. Between lunch and dinner, the hospitality crew, who were mainly from the Philippines and stayed on board for months at a time while we and other voyagers chartered the ship in a series of season's journeys, folded our bunks' top sheets and placed on each of our pillows a flat chocolate wrapped in foil. Yet amid all this luxury came inklings that the comfort was an illusion overlaid upon an unforgiving sea. Before we could proceed north, we executed a mandatory evacuation drill that would teach us what to do in case we were ever forced to abandon ship.

This was a more sobering version of the drill to which air-line travellers have become immune. On a ship's drill a real alarm sounds, loud and insistent and frightening, a sound that penetrates your bones. You don't simply watch an attendant don a life jacket; you find the life jacket in your cabin, put it on and tie its fasteners, then climb to your muster station with the others assigned to your lifeboat. The alarm keeps blaring and there are crackling loudspeakers, and there is wind off the water, and you think about all the shipwrecks you have read about or seen on film or heard about in fire-lit stories, and you know this voyage is not immune to the forces of nature that have made ships like this one disappear — not just in Franklin's time, but recently. This very ship, in fact, had a sister ship which sank, four years before this voyage, on a similar journey through the Antarctic. It took twenty-four hours for it to sink, and all the passengers were saved, but that ship remains at the bottom of the ocean, and to this day no one knows why it failed. Our evacuation drill took about half an hour, and when it was over everyone was glad to take the life jackets off and tuck them back in their hiding places in the cabins, and to relegate the idea of shipwreck to the imagination once again.

After the lifeboat drill we watched Aaju Peter and the other gunbearers load their gear for the time when we might need protection out on the wild land away from houses. Some of us began claiming little territories on the ship, nests where we could hang on to comfort if the encroaching wilderness began to unsettle us. Our captain, a remarkable Swedish man with a demeanour of dignity and composure, appeared on the upper deck with a fishing line whenever the rest of us went onshore, a solitary figure in his red coat fishing for cod or Arctic char that he shared if he made a decent catch. I saw a woman named Heidi take a tiny box of watercolours and paint miniature transparencies of terns, sled dogs, and the pert fireweed blossoms, then slip the paints in her pocket and perform yoga in a quiet corner. Nathan had a pen and his guitar and some paper, and had begun to work on a new song.

"Do you want to look at it?" He handed me the paper with the draft, called "The Turning," scrawled in ink, his own Northwest Passage composition about our ship, about the beauty of the land, and about trying to find comfort in a place where we were all beginning to confront our essential aloneness:

Arctic skies are blue and grey and green
The sun goes down leaving streaks of yellow in between
And I am bound away, north of Hudson Bay
Into a realm where winter winds hold sway
You are here to view the midnight sun
To taste the fruit of tundra where the caribou still run
And the Inuit children play, west of Baffin Bay
And bloom against a tapestry of green and blue and grey

Tonight I put myself to bed with much between us left unsaid
Somehow it's not the way that it should be.
Tonight, alone, I fall asleep with no one here
No one to keep me warm, adrift upon an Arctic sea . . .

Artist Sheena Fraser McGoogan worked on studies and sketches of the optimistic Sisimiut houses whose colours suited her outlook, and held workshops in the ship's library encouraging others to sketch their own chosen subjects. A few passengers who'd never painted before became mesmerized by the alchemy of visual images turning into emotional language. When Sheena's workshops were done I stayed behind: I loved the library, a cozy place with comfy chairs and lots of books on the North. I'd brought my crochet needle and a skein of wool my friend Marilee had given me, spun and hand-dyed by Shawn O'Hagan in Newfoundland, and I began making warm headgear in the library when we weren't exploring in Zodiacs or walking on the land. I saw each passenger retreat to his or her own world while making things, yet after a while we became curious: "What are you making? How are you doing? Did you catch any fish?"

But I longed to leave familiar-looking land behind and enter newness once and for all. I held onto a solitary wish — a desire to see how cold begets loneliness.

I GOT THAT wish the morning I woke to see pieces of iceberg floating outside my porthole. This was the mystery world we had all longed for, yet feared. We wanted, like Nathan in his new song, to venture onto the frozen sea, though we knew it would separate us from all comfort.

As we sailed into Disko Bay, ice floated in silence, quiet green-greys leading to whites and back to blues. There was no sign of any human, only reflections of ice and sky and northern sea, and the light held a low frequency that lent ice and sky and water a glow both incandescent and restrained. This icescape drifted deep in its own thought. The pieces were small and I knew they'd calved from the bigger chunks we'd soon see farther inside Disko Bay as we approached the town named Ilulissat, the Greenlandic word for icebergs. The town rests at the mouth of the fjord that is the birth canal for icebergs born of the Sermeq Kujalleq glacier, greatest mother of ice in the northern hemisphere. So important is it to our planet that in 2004 the Ilulissat Icefjord became a UNESCO World Heritage Site.

As I knelt on my bunk and watched ice float past, I began to feel the electrifying power of the North. This was the moment in our expedition that I first sensed something shift the boundaries between earth and psyche, inner world and external world: the ice floated not outside the ship but within myself. Nothing appearing outside that porthole was finished, in human terms, or built, or completely formed. The icescape was in the process of forming and becoming unformed. It wasn't the ordinary world but a mirror of mind, the origin of forms as we know them. For the first time, I was looking at something not from outside but from within it, in a place that had until now been secret. I was in a hiding place of mysteries.

Facts abound about a place. Of this one, its latitude, the tonnage of icebergs produced in a year, the degrees of change in temperature over past summers, and the geological composition of the fjord that glimmered beyond the floating ice: the scientists and geologists on our voyage provided us with all that. But the emotional reality touched another realm. One

floating soul needed others with whom to respond to the mysterious new languages of land, ice, water — I hadn't before
known earth as a text underlying any word spoken or written
by man. Rather than shying away from others, I moved closer
to the friends I'd begun to make. We were moving into territory occupied by Inuit whose ancestors had, we were told,
come from what we now call Canada. The Northwest Passage, as Europeans conceive of it, has been used as an ice road
by Inuit moving eastward from Alaska for many thousands
of years. People belong to larger territories than we tend to
believe. Rasmussen might have claimed Greenland for the
Danes, but its vast northern reaches remained the habitation
of a circumpolar, nomadic people for whom southern, colonial
ideas of "nationality" were fundamentally irrelevant. I wanted
to hear more of what Aaju Peter had to say about this, as a
Greenlandic woman who had adopted a Canadian Inuit life. I
wanted to ask her about the possibility of "belonging" outside
borders.

"I'm always feeling unmoored from any idea of a homeland," I told her. "I once accidentally let my Canadian passport
expire. But I'd lost my citizenship card, the card they give you
when you swear allegiance to the Queen as a new Canadian."

"You had to swear allegiance to the Queen," Aaju laughed,
"and you were coming from England. See? It's all crazy."

"Yes, and because I'd lost the card, it was much harder for
me to get a new passport than for a born Canadian. Yet when
I visited relatives in the north of England, everyone said I was
no longer one of them."

"I know how that feels," Aaju said.

"They said I'd become Canadian. So I feel sort of at home on the ship, here, between homelands."

"It's perfectly okay," Aaju told me, "to belong to two cultures. Your voice is authentic, because it's human."

TO SEE THE Sermermiut Valley, where the massive Sermeq Kujalleq glacier terminated and began to break into icebergs, we walked through Ilulissat itself. There, the Danish explorer Knud Rasmussen's house had been turned into a museum, and the town had become a centre for the Danish shrimp fishery. I walked uphill past a restaurant called *Moderne Gronlandsk Kokken*—Modern Greenlandic Kitchen—and wished it was Tuesday or Wednesday, when their Greenlandic buffet advertised these offerings:

Reindeer with juniper berry
Braise Musk Ox
Seal steak with bacon and onion
Whale steaks in red wine
Smoked reindeer
Smoked whale
Home dry whale
"Mattaq" (whale skin) and fat

I drooled in front of the sign while others headed uphill. I'd wanted to try *mattaq* for a long time. I knew some people couldn't stand it, but people who loved it said it was sweet and satisfying, better than chocolate, and I knew I'd probably relish it. The food on that list was wild and exciting, and when I finally tore myself away and got to the hilltop behind the others, I was thrilled to see that the *kalaalimineerniarfik*—the fish and meat market—was open. I hurried inside to find it contained plenty of wild food—including cleaned and meticulously arranged carcasses of seal and other sea animals. There were wild murres I recognized from living in outport Newfoundland, and I watched the butcher draw back the wings of a seagull and begin to cut and prepare the meat. In a tub labelled *ammassat* I recognized what Newfoundlanders call caplin.

I'd once lived in an old fisherman's house across from a hidden Newfoundland beach that had a triangular rock pool I used as my bathtub. I bathed among starfish and seaweed. The fisherman's wife, Mary, said that when she was young, that beach was alive with wooden flakes where women dried salt cod, and when they weren't working at the fish or picking berries or digging potato gardens, they looked after animals. "Every woman in the cove," she said, "had her own cow." I bathed there a generation after the heyday she talked about, lying in the sensual silk of rock pool water as waves broke milky froth on the rocks below. The rock bore water marks so sinuous I saw how water had carved curves in the stone. I made up songs in that tub and I suppose, looking back now, the fishermen and their wives might have been unenchanted by my lingering there like some giant white-bellied squid. I could see no windows or houses from the pool, but in retrospect nothing went unnoticed in that village, and I was probably the talk of the town while imagining myself hidden. But one morning, just after the fishermen had gone out in their dories in what was to be the last season before factory trawlers caused cod stocks to plummet beyond all hope, I peeped over my tub and saw caplin rolling in the dawn. The rock-cut below me tumbled with vigorous, wriggling light: tens of thousands of leaping, ovulating, ecstatic pieces of silver. I wrapped my towel around me and climbed down to the sand and into the sea where fish nudged, flickered, and swam over my body. No self-respecting Newfoundlander would watch the caplin run without running to get a bucket, and that's what I did. I filled the bucket with my bare hands, then went home and dipped the fish in flour, sizzled them in oil and devoured them. But better than the devouring were those caplin running over my bare flesh in a silver dawn with no other human around.

Normally the caplin run is a community event. Its day and hour can't be predicted save in a beautiful, time-honoured practice where old men watch the fog and the whales, women gauge mauziness in the air, and children and their dogs play in a pale sun fingering the rocks. June...July...when will the caplin run? It's a question everyone loves; but it has an edge. As long as caplin run, then all has not been changed.

Another village I lived near for years, Brigus, has a tunnel, blasted with gunpowder in the 1800s to let men and goods easily reach the deep-water end of Bartlett's wharf. Near that tunnel is a bit of beach where I once saw caplin come in before the blueberry festival, and it was all about children and their dogs: buckets and buckets of caplin crowded the beach and kids stood on each other's shoulders to wade deeper and scoop fish lying beyond the shallows. This was twenty years after my rock pool days, in a time when kids had started to grow obese from too many quadburgers at the Bay Roberts drive-thru and too much TV and sitting at computers for hours after sitting all day in class. But some of those kids were skinny like they were in the 1960s, like you see in old National Film Board footage of kids on Fogo Island. Kids like sparrows, leaping and flying, kneebones and elbows sharp as penknives unfolding and cutting the water and catching those caplin, shouts ricocheting off the stone tunnel, ringing through it and echoing across plum trees and cherry trees. It was there, it was still alive — the old way of getting wild food from the land — it had not died.

But this lasted one day. The caplin run, like potato gardens and the food fishery, is a flash in the pan — a pan that for many Newfoundlanders now contains fish formed into breaded fillets, "fingers," or "cakes" processed in some offshore factory.

I'd eaten wild food in Newfoundland, but there had been no commercial sale of wild meat in markets — just the same factory-farmed hamburger and sausages as in the rest of North America. Before the codfish moratorium, though, I'd seen murres and puffins in people's freezers. Fishermen caught them as by-catch and, as they afforded protein but were unsaleable by both custom and law, they supplemented a rural family's food supply. It had felt odd to see orange-beaked puffins and other birds I'd thought of as exotic lying rigid among cod fillets, but these were ancient and ongoing food sources, long part of a subsistence economy.

I'd once met my Seal Cove neighbour coming home from his fishing grounds with a lobster hidden under his jacket so neighbours wouldn't see it. Lobster might sell for exorbitant rates in St. John's, but in old Newfoundland communities lobsters were considered a poor man's dish. And no one bought wild meat or fish in a shop. You hunted your own moose, and if you wanted to buy wild caribou sausage you knew which neighbour to go to. If you wanted seal in St. John's, you went down to the waterfront to a truck with "Carcass" and "Flipper" hand-painted on its boards, and you'd better know how to treat the flesh with baking soda and vinegar or you'd have inedible seal and a stench in your kitchen. Processing and eating wild food in Newfoundland was something you did through inherited cultural knowledge, away from markets. To see this thriving Ilulissat fish market was to see the antithesis of how I knew wild food to be treated in eastern Canada. It particularly intrigued me to see a gull being cleaned and cut up for food.

But Aaju wasn't impressed.

"I prefer the Canadian Inuit way," she said as we walked beyond the town, along the trail toward the ice valley.

Here again stood sheds, hung with blue and orange ropes and harnesses for the town's sled dog population, which, at six thousand, outnumbered the human population by fifty percent. The grasses were white with fluffy Arctic cotton grass waving in a wind laced with fresh coolness from the nearby glacier. Motoko, the most glamorous of my cabin mate's Japanese entourage, stopped to pick a tiny Arctic mouse-eared chickweed blossom and thread it in her hair. The flower's elegance struggled to match her own. She wore carmine lipstick and carried a blue parasol.

"Here" — Aaju gestured back toward the fish market — "all that wild meat, they grill it or boil it. They have taken on the Danish way of doing things, and they think the Canadian Inuit practice of eating wild meat or seal or fish raw is primitive." She laughed. "I love to go up to Greenlandic kids and use all my cunning to get them to try raw seal liver, or brain, or heart. They don't want to do it, but then I imply in front of their friends that they're cowards. I shame them into it, and some of them like it. Then they go home and gross out their mothers and fathers. I love doing that."

We walked the trail for a half hour, then reached the stony rise where we could finally see the chaotic jumble of giant ice pieces calving off Sermeq Kujalleq. From high on the rocks it looked and felt to me as if all the ice was waiting — a colossal traffic jam of pieces stalled, jumbled, and crammed against each other, waiting for the sun to melt their edges just enough to erode them and let each one slip away, out of the massive chaos and into a sliding, floating freedom. It was aptly named a calving ground: each broken monolith had laboured down the ice river at a pace — just seven kilometres each year — barely discernible to someone watching; like the hands of a clock, or the movement of stars, or something being born.

The constant repositioning and vying for place gave the ice a pent-up energy that reverberated through the air. It appeared stalled, yet every day between eighteen and twenty million tons of the ice manage to calve off the mother ice river. I found that looking down on the ice made me feel frustrated — I wanted to *see* the movement. The ice's jammed, stalled massiveness reminded me of all the times in my life when I'd felt stalled or blocked. It frustrated me to think of being crammed into such a place, unable to move, waiting until events outside myself—degrees of warmth, the lapping of water—permitted me to move, not of my own volition but purely at the whim of the natural world. I remembered hearing Bernadette Dean whisper about nature's power on the deck of the ship. It baffled her that white Arctic travellers past and present seemed to think themselves more intelligent than the elements.

I did not want to climb down to the low, rocky beach to get a closer look at the jammed ice, but some passengers had done so, and the news filtered uphill that one of them, Motoko—the elegant Japanese woman with her parasol—had twisted her ankle on the stones, and would have to be assisted back to the ship. Marc St-Onge, our geologist, carried her on his shoulders as if she were a princess in a fairy tale: did he feel a personal responsibility, since his beloved rocks had caused the injury? Or did all the male resource staff long for a chance to manifest old-fashioned chivalry? The bearded men took turns carrying Motoko back along the trail. We'd all filled out forms in case we needed special rescue from remote regions, and I wondered if Motoko might be carried off in a helicopter. There was talk that she might have to leave the voyage, and people felt sad: but that evening on the ship, Nathan Rogers carried her upstairs to a barbecue on deck, her foot in a splendid bandage. I remembered what he'd told me about how his father had saved lives on board the plane where he himself had perished: with Motoko hoisted on his shoulders, I sensed Nathan was somehow accompanied by his father in a way even music could not accomplish.

* * *

WE FLOATED BY Zodiac to icebergs gathering at the fjord
mouth: caves, pillars, monumental and illumined with blue
light, and darkness in the deep recesses—so enigmatic and
imposing I said nothing for hours. Were it not for Sheena
McGoogan, who'd begun translating what she saw into her
sketchbooks and encouraged us to do the same, I might have
come away from the whole experience unable to express a
word about it. Only after two years of looking at the images
I sketched, both in the book she gave me and on watercolour
paper, have I been able to speak. I was finding, in the North,
that words are a secondary language: first we see images, then
we feel heat, cold rock, flesh. We taste air before words.

The first words I encountered in the North were made not
through symbols but by rock, sky, and water—and, later, by
the profound animals who possessed potent languages of their
own. In the dramatic gallery of ice that cracked and floated
off the Sermeq Kujalleq glacier into Disko Bay I began to perceive speech and language that proved other than human: to
translate it I'd need to understand my own mind and body in a
new way. This would take coaxing and tutoring by the land we
were to travel, and because I'd been conditioned toward reason, to linear and compartmental thought built by explanation
and deduction, it would take time.

I was far from the first human to lose my bearings here.
Historians call Disko Bay the last place John Franklin was
seen by European eyes. Witnesses claimed they saw him with
his ship moored to an ancestral cousin of the icebergs we were
encountering; once Franklin sailed from Disko Bay, no one
from that part of earth ever saw him again. I felt, on seeing the

icebergs, how one might easily vanish after being in their presence. The idea of mooring one's ship to the ice had a ring of sad folly: had Franklin trusted the ice because of its mass and presence, even though it was made of frozen water and insubstantial as a dream? I tried to picture his ship moored to the ice and felt nothing but surprise at the prospect: both ice and ship seemed destined for dissolution. Might Franklin have sensed this at the outset?

Back on the ship we headed up Karrat Fjord, home to narwhals and seals and colonies of dovekies. We were to go ashore on an uninhabited island, and I saw we were entering a new psychological zone, a hybrid between the urban life we all knew and another, less knowable life ahead. Passengers tried to conjure memories of wilderness hiding within the cities we'd left behind. Surely we knew something about wilderness, about animals? The birders talked with Richard Knapton, the ship's ornithologist, about birds common to both Greenland and their own homes in the south.

"A peregrine falcon," a passenger said, "lives at 2180 Yonge Street in Toronto, on the corner of Yonge and Eglinton. It sits high on the Canadian Tire building, hunts from there, brings prey, and in full view of everyone in the offices, tears it to pieces. Blood everywhere."

"Ravens in Greenland," Richard answered, "will assess the length of a sled dog's chain, then sit just outside of it."

I'd seen those ravens coexisting here with chained huskies. I'd sensed the dogs' haunted spirits cloaking the settlements in resounding howls over the gardens and graveyards. Those dogs tore prey to pieces as well as any peregrine falcon could.

But the land on which we were now about to walk had no dogs and no living humans. There would be human bones, though. The land knew how to devour its share of blood and bone, more ravenous than peregrine or dog.

"Be aware," said Aaron, the young New Zealander who would lead us on our first walk far from any settlement, "that out on the land there are human remains. Respect them, and be aware of the boundary. Notice where the gunbearers are standing. Whatever you do, don't go beyond the gun perimeter."

He sent scouts ashore to establish sightlines and safe hiking places. Aaju and others readied their guns in case we met polar bears.

Marc St-Onge talked of the rocks we were about to walk on as if they were agents of action instead of the stationary lumps I witnessed in the distance. As we approached the rocky island I noticed him getting even more excited than usual.

"The rocks here" — he gesticulated as if at entities that hurtled and tore through space-time — "are all about the collision and suturing of continents."

Marc saw movement where I did not; it amused me, yet I sensed he was trying to transmit a message I couldn't intercept. Rocks, to Marc, were far more powerful than they appeared to me. It wasn't that I doubted Marc's view — but I lacked his perception and could not hear or decipher anything the rocks might be trying to say. I didn't want to even try to hear their language. I was more interested in the ice, water, air, and myriad tiny lichen. On other voyages this ship had brought a botanist along, but we did not have one. I spent a lot of time with my face close to the ground, listening not to Marc's stones, but to the eloquence of diminutive plants. I found their voices exquisite and brave.

We clambered onto a rise where black and orange lichen blazed in perfect circles on the rocks. There were, indeed, human bones, not buried in southern fashion where there is soft ground, but ritualistically lain under cairns of stone that we had to be careful not to disturb. It would have been easy to walk on one if you were negligent, and send rock and fibula and skull tumbling disastrously down the embankment, disturbing spirits. I climbed high over a carpet of tight green moss and minute leaves, and I sprawled on a sun-warmed blanket of turf from where I watched tantalizing icebergs float in the distance, breaking off into smaller and smaller pieces that floated then melted in the water with a fluid serenity. I was elated to have a vantage point no other passenger had found, though it meant I lay near the bones of a long-dead hunter reclining under a stone mound.

I lay alongside those bones on top of the stony ridge, listening to the soundscape. On our ship our captain once again fished from his deck, a distant figure raising and lowering his single line while around him roared a crashing boom as icebergs cracked and avalanched. The fjord acted as an orchestral chamber, magnifying the sounds of these ice monoliths as they crushed and worked. It sounded like a vast construction site. There was a gunshot crack, then a thump and another avalanche; layered under these were the lapping of water, the echoing roar of wind around the moonscape mountains, and other, more distant collisions of ice echoing down the fjord. I climbed higher and found a rock shelf. I sat on the ledge in one place for a long time, alone and listening.

chapter six

THE CAPTAIN

WE WOKE THE next day in Upernavik, halfway up Greenland's west coast and not possessed of ice-free waters or any
substantial spring thaw, though its name means "springtime
place." Here the graveyard protects its dead above ground,
like the graves we'd just seen in Karrat Fjord — boulders had
been piled to cover the bodies, and now moss softened the
stones. The village of 1,100 is home to fishers and hunters of
polar bear and seal. Men came out to watch us as we walked
up the road through the village, whose houses, like those we'd
seen farther south, were neat and bright — yellow and blue
and green and red, with sharp white contrasting trim. The
dogs here howled in unison at the noon whistle — no matter
where they were in the community, they remained connected
as a pack. Their harnesses hung alongside relics of past hunts
from hooks and nails in sheds along the road.

Danny Catt, the ship's photographer, nodded to a shaft of

old bone several feet long, hanging in a shed doorway he and I happened to pass together. "Do you know what that bone is?"

"No."

"That, Kathleen, is a walrus penis bone."

Inshore boats had docked in the bay where a man named Peter had just come in with a seal. The animal lay splayed on flat stones and its blood glazed many square yards of rock which shone red in the mist. Peter offered his eight-inch blood-stained knife to Laura, one of the younger women on board. He was shy and he offered it silently, dangling it with grace and a daring invitation.

He'd already split the seal's belly-fat and opened the skin and the attached inch-thick blubber like two halves of an open coat. In the bloody V-shaped opening I saw harmony: the precise and ordered arrangement of innards, dark rib-bones slanting like beams of a ship, and the dense heart-engine studding the centre of it all. The small and large intestines beautifully frilled around each other, pale and coiled and somehow joyous in their tangle of connectedness. Laura plunged in and did what Peter shyly indicated, getting her arms bloodstained to the elbows.

Aaju asked Peter, "Can you collect some parts for me?" She gave him a Ziploc bag. "Can you collect some blood?" Peter poured blood into the bag and stood holding it over the reddened stones. The stones were slippery and I skidded and fell on them as I strained to get a closer look.

"Brain?" asked Aaju. "Heart? Could I please take a piece of liver?"

As Laura dismantled the seal, piling up ribs, flippers, and

other sections in neat categories, Aaju hunkered with Bernadette Dean and picked out morsels and ate them there on the
stones, their fingers covered in blood. Aaju wrapped precious
pieces and brought them, with the blood, on board the ship to
prepare and share later. She picked sweet, black crowberries
and mixed them, later on the ship, with the white seal brain,
until the whole mass looked like stirred blueberry yogurt. I ate
some and again, like the liver she'd shared in the oil lamp ceremony, I was surprised it tasted so mild and sweet.

Later, I'd stay out on deck until 3 a.m. in the silver-blue
luminosity of the Arctic night. It felt as if the North were holding light and saving it for parts of the world that lay in darkness. I didn't understand how anyone could sleep through such
mystery and power.

THE NEXT DAY in my cabin there sat a card inviting me to
dine with the captain. I'd dined once before with a captain,
and knew it to be a special occasion. My other captain was
from my husband's hometown, and his ship sailed regu-
larly between Montreal and St. John's. Docked in St. John's,
Mathieu had invited Jean and me onboard. I learned four
things. The first was that while Mathieu's ship came to Newfoundland laden — with stoves, fridges, tins of beans, pairs of
jeans and winter coats, bricks and boards, parasols and ten-
inch nails — it left empty. The second was that the vessel must
never, ever be called a boat, but always a ship. The third was
that a ship's engine room is a marvel of clanking painted geometric dangerous beautiful surfaces, corners, and gangplanks,

and treacherous bridges and stairs and perilous handrails that make me dizzy with their massive impenetrability and importance. And the fourth was that while everyone else on a ship may be having bacon and gingerbread for lunch, the captain and his guests begin with prime rib and end with something called a profiterole: a confection made of layers of air-light pastry piped full of fresh cream and enrobed in chocolate.

I mentally thanked Denise for instructing me to pack a little black dress. I had a good relationship with that dress. Sleeveless with a plunging neckline, it swished around my knees like a black petunia. I was uncertain about this sort of dress on the trip, however. Concerned with observing, I had no wish to be observed, especially not in any way hinting at glamour, but I could hardly show up at the captain's table in my alpaca vest, long johns, and the jeans I'd found on the sidewalk in front of Jean Coutu Pharmacy. I rinsed my blue flip-flops, each tipped with a plastic chrysanthemum, and hoped my super-short haircut would counteract any perception that I might be looking for romance. I considered the crocheted beard I'd shoved in my suitcase; it covered my chin nicely and I thought it looked fairly distinguished, but I did not think I should wear it to the captain's dinner.

At lunch our rear admiral announced that in honour of our recent time in Disko Bay, and to give us plenty to do as we set off on our sea-crossing to the Canadian Arctic—a journey that would stretch overnight and through the better part of the following day as we traversed Davis Strait—dinner that night would be followed by a disco in the forward lounge.

"I can't wait," Nathan told me as he passed with a plate

of bison balls and watermelon. "I've brought a special outfit. I'll be wearing bell-bottoms and silver lamé. You're coming, right?"

"I...um..."

"Come on, dude, you have to go to the disco."

"Feel free," the rear admiral announced, "to ignore any of our activities that fall into the category of Clearly Stupid. Don't forget the upcoming Arctic Plunge. Anyone who jack-knifes into Lancaster Sound will earn an *Arcticus Feverus* patch and the Green Glove of Courage. And sharpen your pencils for our Limerick Competition, immediately following dinner — whoever writes the most immensely stupid limerick might win the second prize of a bottle of Bowmore single malt scotch to share with the miserable losers."

I leaned over to Gillian, a British passenger with whom I was lunching for the first time, and confessed I wasn't much of a party animal.

"I'm a fan of single malt," I told her, "but not of discos. I might have to retire to the serenity of my cabin."

"I think I'll have to go to the disco. My cabin is out of bounds for the moment." She waved a forkful of Arctic char and chanterelles. Gillian had, during our first course of turtle bisque, become excited when I told her I'd been invited to have dinner that night with the captain. She argued when I'd confided that, at fifty, I now considered myself to be invisible to men.

"Not yet," she'd said, arching her brows and fixing me with a meaningful stare. "You are most decidedly not yet invisible."

Like the other resource staff, I sat with different passengers at each meal. It was part of my work to listen and share in their stories—hardly a difficult job for me, since I loved listening. But it turned out that I also ended up sharing my own secrets with strangers. Something about sailing toward the Northern ocean made for easy storytelling—we were funnier and more vulnerable; we were just passing acquaintances, yet the ship lent us intimacy and it felt exciting.

"Why is your cabin out of bounds?" I asked Gillian.

"There's a man with his head down our loo."

"*There's a man with his head down our loo!*" I chanted. "That would be perfect in the limerick contest."

"Did he say the *second* prize is a bottle of scotch? I wonder what the first prize is."

"I heard a rumour that it's a pair of skin-tight scarlet underpants." I'd been listening during a limerick organizers' confab earlier, in one of the corridors.

"Underpants," Gillian roared. Geologists at the next table paused in their discussions of unconformities, time-gaps, and crystalline basements to glance our way. "Don't talk to me about underpants. Especially not underpants on ocean voyages."

"Why not?"

"I was twenty-one. It was my first transatlantic voyage and I was pleased with myself for having had the foresight to fit myself out with disposable knickers."

One geologist was having a hard time focusing on the Paleozoic Arctic platform. He tilted toward our conversation while his companions got excited about something older rocks had done to younger rocks 542 million years ago.

"Disposable knickers?" I popped a chanterelle in my

mouth and tried to ignore our eavesdropper. Ignoring is one of my mother's tactics.

"They were made of paper. They were the *latest* thing."

I imagined disposable knickers in the windows of Harrods and Selfridges. It was a fad my mother had not mentioned. But Gillian was younger than my mother. Disposable knickers might have occurred during my mother's child-rearing years without her notice, the way I'd failed to notice thongs in the nineties.

"Weren't they uncomfortable?"

"I don't remember. I just remember how pleased I was with myself for having a fresh pair each day that I could wear and then toss in the wastebasket."

"It meant you had more room for souvenirs."

"That was one benefit. But the cabin boy, seeing my disposable knickers in the wastebasket, took it upon himself to *restore* them."

"Restore?"

"He rescued them out of the wastebasket and folded them neatly at the foot of my bed."

AS DINNER APPROACHED I felt nervous. I was a bit afraid of the Swedish captain but at the same time intrigued. He had magnificent white hair and brass buttons. Everyone said he was the best captain with whom they'd ever had the good fortune to sail; expert at navigating ice, shoals, and treachery of all kinds around Spitsbergen and the Norwegian Sea and Antarctica as well as the territory we were to cover. Every dinner hour he walked slowly and sat with gravity at his table with the ship's doctor and chief engineer. He drank cognac and gave off an air I found both imposing and dear, since I perceived he might sometimes feel lonesome.

Now, at the dining room's head table, I was relieved to find other passengers had been invited to dine with the captain too — a mother and daughter named Nancy and Anne; the rear admiral himself; Heidi, whom I'd watched painting delicate watercolours; and two other women at the starboard side whose names I did not catch. But I was seated beside the captain, his uniform grazing my bare arm.

His buttons glittered and as he bought me a cognac that also glittered, I felt an acceleration of something I'd begun noticing in my life on land just before arriving on the ship. By the time you've had a couple of marriages and children who've grown or almost grown, you've been through a machine that sucks in young people and spits out officially certified grownups. There could be nothing more grown up, I thought, than this table with its captain, the rear admiral, and other elegant guests. Yet... did I sense we were all play-acting? I felt a suppressed hilarity, yet nobody wanted to speak first. We were all a little intimidated by the grand uniform. And the captain was a reserved man.

"Vikings," he finally announced. "The word 'Vikings' refers to 'the bay.' The V is the shape of a bay, and so 'V-Kings' were 'Kings of the Bay.' They lived and hid there, for strategic reasons."

This was news to me. I found it funny that the captain saw the "V" in Viking as a picture — a hieroglyph — instead of a letter. Might he be joking? Here above the Arctic Circle I was a world away from my *Oxford Dictionary of English Etymology*. I missed it now, edited by someone called C. T. Onions. For a person adept at peeling layers of language, Onions was a name improbable as Kings of the Bay, yet it was really the man's name. How outrageously the captain's buttons glittered! I thought again of *The Jumblies*:

> *And each of them said, "How wise we are!*
> *Though the sky be dark, and the voyage be long,*
> *Yet we never can think we were rash or wrong*
> *While round in our Sieve we spin!"*

The captain's pronouncement on Vikings and bays was his only comment during the entire dinner. Perhaps he had been serious.

His solitude felt imposing and silent. In sitting close to him I understood him to possess a great deal more gravity than I did. I perceived that a captain is an ambassador of land in the territory of water. He lends his ship earthly presence that the water recognizes and — if he's a good captain — respects. To come to a conclusion on any matter, he spends more time waiting, watching, and weighing circumstances than ordinary people do. I'd see him do just this throughout the voyage, observing from the deck, or on the sidelines of gaiety on board the ship, and I felt that his practice of solitary fishing from the bridge might be a comfort to him; that he loved the land, ice, and wildlife that lived without words. Why did he love a body as fluid as the ocean? Because she held him in an engagement that did not require him to respond to human pettiness but connected him with the gravitas she herself embraced.

After dinner I escaped downstairs and lay on my bunk intending to skip the disco, but I heard music coming from the floors above and thought about how much I love dancing. I love flinging my flip-flops under a table and dancing barefoot half the night. I even like slow dances, as long as my partner doesn't try anything involving coordinated upraised arms, and the captain, I was sure, would not spring Hollywood pyrotechnics on anyone.

I went back upstairs and edged into the crowd around the dance floor. On the other side, once more in the margins, stood the captain, his eyes vivid blue even in the dark.

When I ask someone to dance I lose all fear. Dancing doesn't mystify me like small talk at parties or conversations with other mothers in parent-teacher lineups. In Montreal, the artist Sherwin Sullivan Tjia holds slow-dance nights full of strangers, and I sometimes go alone. Sherwin, in his heels and strapless gown, provides dance cards and invites designated dancers in golden vests to dance with wallflowers for the first few sets, and by midnight we're all strangers no more.

I strode through red and orange lights toward the captain, who stood dignified, silent, and—by obvious choice—in shadow, beyond the sweep of the glittering colours.

"Would you"—where did I get the brazenness?—"Would you like to dance?"

But the captain said, "I do not dance."

"Never?"

"No."

"That's a pity."

"It might be a pity, but it is the truth."

I didn't feel offended or embarrassed. I knew he meant what he said, and I thought perhaps it made sense that he didn't dance: he spent his days and nights navigating the waves, an all-encompassing waltz with the whole planet, more exhilarating than any song on a wooden floor and so lifelong he had no space left on his dance card.

The ship's engineer was a shy Scottish man who appeared at the ends of corridors carrying a wrench and wearing white overalls. He was never far from the captain and he'd seen the captain refuse to dance with me. He stepped forward now in a gallant gesture that managed to ask my permission to dance while it rescued me from having to sit or dance alone. I've never seen a man take a woman by the waist so gently and dance with such assurance and in such lovely sympathy with the music, as if he'd been dancing most of his life and hardly ever wearing overalls or carrying a wrench, and that hand around my waist heated right through my dress.

It reminded me that my mother and father had met at a dance. They had, in their seventies, just shared the story with me.

"Your dad was a good dancer," said my mother.

"That's nice," I said. "Neither of my husbands can dance at all."

"Slow dances, I mean. Foxtrots and waltzes and the like."

"Dancing with each of my husbands has been like trying to dance with a two-hundred-pound sack of potatoes."

"Well, your dad knew how to dance beautifully and so did

his friends. I guess they just had it in them somehow, naturally. Maybe it was the era."

My dad had come into the room and heard this.

"Had it in us naturally?" He started to snort.

"Well, I don't know how you knew it," my mother said, getting in a huff.

In the black-and-white photo, my mother wears pencil heels and a smashing dress with a flared skirt. You can tell she's a redhead and her lipstick is carmine. Dad is looking very hipster in a suit with skinny lapels; his hair's sticking up and he's got serious glasses like the young people all wear now in Montreal. There's a Christmas tree behind them and they both sparkle, ready to whirl off in each other's arms as soon as someone spins the latest Frankie Laine.

"We knew how to dance," my dad said, "because me and Joe Cramm used to go for lessons every Friday night. All the boys did, after we found out there was this beautiful dance teacher who let us plant our hands right on her hips so she could demonstrate. We never missed a single lesson." He giggled his way into the kitchen to compress bread, cheese, and onion in the sandwich toaster.

"You never knew he'd taken lessons?"

"No," my mother said. "I never ever knew that."

Maybe our shy, Scottish ship's engineer had taken lessons too. I was having a hard time getting used to a new realization: any men who might ask me to dance were not young, and this had been the case for longer than I'd been aware. Being married with children stunts your perception of your sensual self — at least it had stunted mine. Maybe other people do not go to the hairdresser and feel astonished to see hair that was brown in the morning change to grey as it falls on the floor.

I had no trouble noticing that other people were growing old, but the retreat of my own youth glared at me on our journey. I was glad I was far from home so I could think about it and maybe come to some more realistic self-image than the one I'd held onto since my late twenties, and which was now far from accurate despite British Gillian's assertion that I hadn't yet become invisible. I might not mind learning how to become old if I could approach the territory with some sort of decent plan. But what if such a plan was like the charts and maps our captain consulted on this Northwest Passage journey: part wish, part fabrication—subjective and incomplete?

As the dancers dwindled and dispersed to their beds, I took to the deck, hanging over the rail and watching the silver-blue wake as we headed northwest, away from Greenland and toward the fabled passage.

chapter seven

BODIES OF WATER

GREENLAND HAD INTRIGUED me, but I was excited to leave
its shores: to leave it meant the ship was about to embark,
finally, for that dreamscape European history calls the Northwest Passage. Greenland's ancient icefjords might be the birth
canal of northern ice, but we'd remained in its southern part,
full of Danish influence and villages that resembled places
I'd known. It thrilled me to leave that land behind; to set out
across Baffin Bay, on no land. I stood on the back deck and
watched the wake all night, grey-white plume on grey-white
sea, with the sky above turning that shade of Arctic half-light
that never loses luminescence. There was a wakefulness in my
heart that would not become sleepy no matter how late the
hour according to any clock. In this I was like a child who
won't acquiesce to bedtime, but who hangs on the banister in
her pyjamas—the mysteries of a wakeful night so much more
thrilling than a dream. Our ship approached an aspect of the

New World to which my father had longed to bring our family when I was a child, but we were taking a route that opened not onto Newfoundland streets, nor upon any New World dream of my father's, but into a whole other realm.

For some pilgrims, wanderlust carries its own seed of disillusion, but for my father I don't think it did. My mother frequently lets slip some comment about how life doesn't turn out the way we dream it might when we're young. But my father never says anything like this, and I wonder if it's because, for him, the reality of life in Canada is no different from the way he'd envisioned it as a young man.

My mother had a lifelong dream of going to the Metropolitan Opera in New York City. She sang in our house every Saturday afternoon during live radio broadcasts from the Met: through vents in the kitchen, the laundry room, and my purple bedroom came her robust renditions of arias from *La Traviata* and *La Bohème* as she hung clothes and rolled pastry while my father went hunting with a Mi'kmaq friend in much the manner Samuel Hearne had documented in his Coppermine treks a hundred years before Franklin. Not that I ever saw my father cut venison strips, sun-dry them, hammer them to powder, or subsist on them until spring. He liked my mother's Cornish pasties very much.

"Mam," I asked, when we'd finally been to the Met together and I realized that all through my youth she'd belted out a contralto as fine as any we'd heard onstage, "did you ever want to be a real opera singer? I mean, at some point when you were young, did you think you might be able to . . ."

"Yes."

She consulted her Cadbury Milk Tray with new intensity. It bore a map pinpointing the coordinates of Turkish Delight, Orange Truffle, Nut Secret, and Honey Love, a guide she preferred to my father's topographical charts of the Newfoundland interior where salmon ran and moose rutted. If a box of chocolates contained no map of its contents my mother would disdain it; but the more uncertain the boundaries of any stretch of Newfoundland muskeg, the more my father rejoiced. We lived nothing like our neighbours, who ate Kraft Squeez-A-Snak and mini marshmallows and dwelt in little boxes made of ticky-tacky from the Malvina Reynolds song my father sang (along with other American protest songs and the entire oeuvre of Hank Williams) when my mother was not filling the halls with Verdi or Puccini.

There were certain New World things our family tried together, without help from anyone actually born west of the Atlantic. I came home from school to find my mother sitting in Dad's armchair, biting a green pepper as if it were an apple. Stony-faced, she crunched it, pith, seeds, and all, to give it a real chance in her mind. This was her formal introduction to a New World vegetable that had not crossed her path in any form in South Shields.

Soon after we immigrated, my father decided to drive us from Newfoundland to British Columbia and back, to see all of Canada and know what we were getting into. I remember endless stones, blue conifers, and a New Brunswick road that was supposed to make us feel we were going uphill while going down. (It didn't make me feel that way at all; no one could explain why I felt the wrong thing and I became deeply uneasy about New Brunswick.) We passed a lot of fields with giant seed parcels pressing right up against the highway, prepared to obliterate sojourners in a smothering mass of leaning stalks with great bulges and intimidating hairs that stood at attention, ready to attack.

"That," said my father, "is corn."

He stopped the car. We got out, and he instructed each of us how to pick a piece of corn. "They are called ears," he said, "and you peel them like this...then you eat the kernels." We ate the raw corn and I felt its starchy-sweet, gritty milk in my mouth, and again I wondered at a place where green peppers with their bitterness and corn with its sticky incompleteness were considered normal food. I'd puzzled unhappily over peanut butter, which every Corner Brook kid appeared to live on— it stuck my mouth shut, and made me shudder the way Brussels sprouts did. It never occurred to me that my mother had bought the wrong brand, or that my parents were making up their own story of how to be Canadian as we went along, from things they'd read and perhaps from hearsay my father gleaned in the staff room of the junior high school where he taught woodwork. There was a missing element, the element that occurs when you're aware of local customs and how to cook the food and find the food in the first place, or how to go outdoors and be Canadian in *this* century, not two centuries ago. I think now that my parents were brave, and that they learned how to be Canadian after they'd become adult, which was harder than it was for their kids. When Newfoundland fishermen asked me, "Where do you belong?" I could never bring myself to give them a straight answer.

It was our aloneness I remember: the singularity of our
small family out in my father's beloved Newfoundland wilderness, which is still there and really exists, but which was for
us something different than it was for others who lived there.
How else to explain why we were the only family in the blueberry grounds, or why we stayed there from dawn to dusk
getting covered in mosquito bites, no other family in sight,
until we each filled a five-gallon pail? How else to account
for the bitterly cold days we spent on George's Lake on Sears
skates, teetering over the bumps with collapsing ankles until
we skated something — but not quite — like our classmates on
the rink at Humber Gardens?

My father led us through the woods for hours on cross-
country skis we'd Minwaxed in the basement to suit snow he
deemed crusty or wet or powdered or sticky or any one of the
things he told us snow might be. Or we hiked on snowshoes
made from wood he cut, heated, and bent, hissing, in buckets
of water, the laces made of sinew from his own moose. If we
lost one of my brothers the rest of us called out, backtracked,
and dug through drifts and snow-laden firs. Our coats were
too thin — the wind blew through them — and our knitted
mittens hung with balls of ice, but we were Canadians.

At our log cabin, a sandy inlet had a boulder where I sat to
play my plastic flutophone. I went to the edge with my lonely
whistle by some instinct that said one body of water might
be replenished by a larger one. I tried "Plaisir d'amour," but
because sad songs in minor keys were too much for a flutophone, I ended up regaling the loons with the cancan from
Orpheus in the Underworld. I didn't know it then but I was stuck

on Jane Franklin's era, songs she'd have heard whenever she was able to tear herself away from the telegraph office seeking reports of her lost husband: Hector Berlioz arranged "Plaisir d'amour" for orchestra in 1859, the year Jane found out the scandalizing details of her husband's death—cannibalism!—and *Orpheus in the Underworld* was first performed the year before. As I played, the others ate peanuts and played hangman by Coleman lantern at the table my father had made, by the fireplace he'd built from boulders that had once accompanied my stone chair.

The loons were unearthly. I did not love the birds, the hills, the lake, the cabin, or the wilderness to which my father had brought us. The mosquitoes were mechanical giants, each burrowing a needle in my arm while I watched its belly balloon to greatness, red with my blood. I liked to wait till the thing had gorged itself giant, then splat it so a smattered poppy of red with a dead, black body in it lay flat on my skin. This was an alien land, these were alien bloodsuckers, the loons a reminder that unfamiliar life populated this place to which my dad had come. Our outhouse tormented me: when I went in there I held my breath, so tortured was I by its fruity stink and knockout punch of ammonia. When I burst back out into fragrant fir and spruce I felt dizzy and faint, failing to understand our family's version of the New World in the 1970s.

Why did no other families live as we did? And how was it that our lake, and the rivers full of trout where my dad and brothers kayaked, held no allure for me? This was a place whose floral emblem, the pitcher plant, was carnivorous, trapping passing insects in its cache of stagnant water in order to

devour them. My grandmother had been right: the wilderness
here would drown you. It sucked your body into itself and
made you disappear. Its crackerberry flowers, with their white
shout of four petals then their carmine scream as the berries
bloomed, were just one word from a land whose message was
not for me. For my father the land spoke, and he was glad in
it. But maybe that's how it is with Old World men, who don't
understand what the New World's acid soil, or its medicinal
shock of wind and Labrador tea, might do to the humours of
their daughters.

Tortured junipers cling to Newfoundland's coast, clasping
the green clifftops like blackened silver claws. Bodies of water
had touched me gently in the Old World. The River Tyne,
crane-lined as it was, full of chemical pollutants left from the
industrial age and causing epidemics of thyroid disease in
northeast England, had yet been my own river. It had brought
ships' twinkling lights into my childhood bedroom. Stories of
my father carrying a goat in a barrow along its banks, or having Guinness picnics with my mother on the worn grass, or
carving a door in our back fence for a dog named Cassius, had
been my stories, unlike those of the new-found land's meat-
eating plants, or its girl-swallowing bog horrors and loon
music. The North Sea might have had stupid beaches peopled
with too many goose-pimpled children in sand shoes who
didn't know what a hot dog was and whose fishing adventures
yielded no more than a tadpole in a jam jar, and maybe you did
have to pay twenty pence for a striped deck chair and a piece of
sand the size of a postage stamp, but it had been my North Sea.
I didn't know how to connect with the Atlantic Ocean around

Newfoundland's coast. My father might have loved that it was bigger and wilder than the North Sea, and that he could freely dig for clams and mussels, but what did that mean to me, since we were always the only people on any beach to which he took us, and there was no one but our own lost English unit to confide in, or laugh with, or love?

Now, crossing Baffin Bay by night, I asked myself about dreamland. Had my father, had all expatriates from the Old World, come to the New World in a kind of dream? Had they followed illusions, led on by rivers, lakes, and seas? Had the River Tyne, reflecting its industrial lights, dazzled me into believing in fairyland, and did stars and the aurora borealis reflect on oceans to wink at and delude sailors in order to drown their bones? Was the least navigable body of water the human body, with its liquid blood, tears, and dreams sloshing around inside, and had Baffin Bay deluded Franklin and all the colonial explorers before him into thinking a northwest passage would lead to the Orient, to spices and bejewelled delights no one in their right mind should believe in, and would not have believed in, were it not for the intolerable dreariness and smallness of England?

On the deck of our ship I wondered if the diffuse glory I'd glimpsed in my youth might not be just another example of how dreamland has forever beguiled us. It wasn't the first time I'd been on a transcontinental ship. In my twenties I'd asked the officers of a Newfoundland fluorspar freighter headed for England if I could pay for passage aboard their vessel. I knew they took occasional passengers, but I didn't know until too late that you had to be a man. They refused to take me. So I found a pair of coveralls hanging in the cloakroom, waited for dusk, and slipped aboard the vessel, where I lay for a couple of hours under tarps and ropes and barrels, hoping to wake up on the open sea. Had I not asked first, I might have succeeded as a stowaway, but someone in the office had spied me hanging around earlier in the day, and they searched the ship pretty thoroughly and sent me on the road. I hitched a ride to Gander airport and flew by midnight plane to Newcastle, looked after my blind grandfather for a couple of weeks, ate Yorkshire pudding and mushy peas in seaside pubs, and boarded the Paris-Naples express to follow to their catastrophic conclusions some long-held illusions of my own.

As I thought of all these things on my night watch, I sensed a secrecy about our navigation across Baffin Bay. We were changing continents without fanfare; going from the Old World to the beaches of the New. The North's permanent twilight obscured a shift from one geography's psychology to the completely different atmosphere of a new land. As morning suffused clarity into the already luminous night, we entered the meandering straits Europeans had named the Northwest Passage, a name as wishful and fatal as it was entrancing.

AT BREAKFAST MARC St-Onge told me how parts of the Geological Survey of Canada's stunning new map of northern minerals came to be made.

"Two hunters," he said, "noticed a wink of blue stone."

"Hunters?"

"Yes, we consult with hunters, with local people, all the

time. The hunters saw the sapphires and told our geologists, and the geologists confirmed the find. That's how we know of many of the minerals that appear on the new map."

"But doesn't the discovery of sapphires and all those other gems and minerals endanger people's hunting grounds?" I was thinking of mines, roads, refineries, tailings ponds, and all those industry-related developments from which sapphires winking under the northern lights seemed so far removed. "Isn't making a map of northern minerals a precursor to taking land away from Northern people?"

"Geology isn't concerned," he said, "with taking land from anybody, or wielding power over the people who live on the land being studied. Geologists concern themselves with pure knowledge. We find out what exists. Mapping it is nothing but a way of transferring that knowledge to the federal government, and to other people who might have an interest."

"But can you say there's such a thing as pure knowledge that doesn't have a point of view, or an agenda, or a power dynamic that'll change the land and the way local people can live on it and use it?"

"The new Geological Survey map," he replied, "might give local people an opportunity; a new way, perhaps, of living a Northern life that remains connected to the land."

I realized I wasn't going to find a comfortable perch at either end of this argument. I gave Marc, who had a cold, one of my nasty but effective Vogel echinacea tablets and went back out on deck, thinking of the hunters who had been the first to notice that wink of blue stone. Where were they now? Were they still able to hunt on the gem-studded land? Had they

been paid for their work as consultants to the mining industry, or had they shared their knowledge and discoveries as an
informal, human interaction like sharing news of weather and
ice conditions? It made me think of Gretel Ehrlich's account,
in *This Cold Heaven*, of meeting Uutaaq, a hunter whose father
had accompanied Robert Peary on his February 1909 polar
expedition.

"Most of the Inuit who went to the pole with Peary weren't
really paid when they got back," Uutaaq told Ehrlich. "Peary
just thanked them. He gave my father some carpenter's tools.
It's hard to know how people thought then, but without the
local people here, Peary would never have had any success."

IT'S NOT EVERY day a place retains the potency it had when it
represented a dream or a wish. In front of me now stood mountains that something nameless had imagined out of crumpled
light and the glow of sapphires. Namelessness had breathed
substance into the light the way it had breathed breath into
man, as if human bodies and the body of this land were
negative versions of each other: man, a breath-containing
substance; the North, a substance-imbued breath.

The colours burned cold and intense — that turquoise
Arctic water, the snow, ice, and purple mountains — and I felt
the complete *presence* of a terrain that knows an absence of the
markers that signify "business as usual" in the south. Light
did not contain itself within southern boundaries, but sank
into the water and land and made them glow. Light pulsed in
and out of rock, ice, and water, illumining strange crevices.
This illumination entered my mind and cast light on thoughts

hiding in shadows, and entered my body too, the same energy imbuing the land. My whole being became ignited in a hybrid world between thought and material process.

Elisabeth joined me. She, along with Nathan Rogers, was one of the few people I ever encountered on the middle deck. Before I'd spoken with Marc at breakfast that morning, I'd seen her sitting in the dining room, demurely holding a piece of what looked like rolled-up lace, and I'd asked her about it.

"This," she'd murmured, leaning in so no one else could hear, "is my thirty-year-old woollen undergarment."

"May I please see it?"

There are people in my life who make me feel coarse next to their composure and fineness. Elisabeth was steeped in grace, yet clearly possessed a funny bone I was eager to yank. I sensed mischief about her, as if she'd escaped the borders of a confining aristocracy like someone from a Jane Austen novel, or Jane Austen herself—except with an exquisite French accent.

"You want me to reveal my thirty-year-old woollen undergarment, here, in the dining room of the ship?" She held it securely on her knees and looked around at the white tablecloths and glinting water glasses.

"Come on!" I reminded myself of my mother, who'd once entered a shop and exclaimed to the proprietor—whom she knew only through having had her assistance in developing our family photos—in front of all the other customers, "Oh, you look wonderful. Now why is that? Well! It's because you've got yourself some new teeth!" I didn't want to emulate my mother in the outlandish personal announcements department, but we can't help being like our mothers some-times. At least I tried to keep my voice down. "I'm dying to see it."

Elisabeth made sure no one was watching as she unrolled the garment upon her lap as if it were parchment. Of web-fine wool, it possessed long sleeves ending in demure, shirred edges, a scalloped neckline, and a pattern of wild roses. It looked like something Lady Franklin might have worn.

"I've never seen anything like it."

"No?"

"It has eyelets, and is so fine, yet made all of wool. Woollen lace! And the colour . . ."

"It is that colour because it is ancient," she said. "It was white when it was in its original condition, believe it or not. Now it is . . . it has gone *beyond*." She rolled it up with deft haste. I got the impression that, while she believed I truly thought the garment beautiful, she felt no one in her right mind would regard it so. Other diners would think it uncouth for her to have it laid out on her knees whilst they lopped the tops off soft-boiled eggs and slipped plum confit onto spoons. I got the idea that while Elisabeth cherished the garment in private, in public she felt bound to claim she was ashamed of it. I loved her for this, and I wanted to look at the garment again, but sensed she didn't want it exposed a second longer. What if it fell under the scrutiny of someone who didn't understand it had once been beautiful, or how faithful it had been through thirty Canadian winters?

"It has long sleeves," I marvelled.

"Yes."

"The wool's so fine it's like a spiderweb."

"Fine, yet very warm."

"Do you think," I said, "it might be possible for you to lend me the garment so I can draw it?"

"You want to make a drawing of my ancient underwear?"

"I do."

She was reluctant, but in the end I persuaded her to let me record the romance of the old woolen lace. I took it and put it in my cabin next to my sketch journal, and I intended to spend time with it in the library at night, recording its delicateness with my pencils.

But now we were on the deck, coming into Pond Inlet, and I was glad of Elisabeth's restraint because I wouldn't have wanted either of us to speak as the ship entered this world of effervescent newness: turquoise water, purple and gold mountains, white mist. It was like being inside a wish, and was in fact that very thing, for wasn't the entrance to the Northwest Passage the essence of what my father and Englishmen before him had wished, gazing from cramped Britain toward sapphires and silk roads in what they called the Orient? And I had somehow, yearning to follow my own filament of something elusive and glimmering, oriented myself into the centre of the wish: here were myself and Elisabeth, alone on the deck of a ship, immersed in it.

There's a space between desire and fruition, idea and being, wishing and consummation, and I recognized that territory. It's the gap in which a child asks, "Are we there yet?" It was the thing I was searching for when I went alone, in my twenties, to Naples on an express train from Paris after my stowaway attempt. In Naples I watched fishermen throw their live catch into crates, and walked alleys where women hollered from windows as they lowered baskets of laundry and tomatoes. I'd stayed in a hotel whose courtyard had casements out of which flew passionate arguments, chairs, lamps, tables with the tablecloths still on them, all plummeting to the cobblestones. "Are we there yet?" I asked a Neapolitan lover and an Egyptian pursuer offering a white box tied with a ribbon I never did open — Naples was a dangerous city from which I escaped in time, but in that danger I reached for a place of immersion and belonging that existed for others but not for me.

Everyone longs for a secret door, an opening to a world beyond loneliness — it's part of the human imagination. But stand under the lowering baskets in Naples all you want — you can't climb in, or be the women lowering them or the youths catching them and hoisting them to market. And these Arctic hills, gold, blue, and purple, were achingly remote: our ship floated past and they lay just beyond reach. Each breath was a cold shock and the land was magnetic, like an encounter with someone who truly sees you: yet we were offshore.

"It looks so . . . unattainable," I said, gripping the white rails.

"'Unattainable.'" Elisabeth savoured the word with restrained laughter.

Perhaps she was a woman who had no desire to attain anything. If she and I were both starving and we sat at a table on which someone placed a delectable piece of roast meat, I'd pounce on it, whereas Elisabeth could sit with her hands folded for an eternity, not eating a morsel unless it was proffered by the person responsible for its appearance. She wouldn't even *look* hungry.

"But it's —" I grappled. "The land, it's *doing* something."

Elisabeth held an affinity with the moment and her silence was a response.

I knew the land wasn't sitting inert. It was acting on us, and I was unprepared. The land was a companion, alive. It had something to say, but we were too far off. It whispered and had a body. I hadn't known land had a body, or was a body, though people are forever saying "a body of land" or, for that matter, "a body of water." I'd thought it a figure of speech, but now I remembered the words "figure" and "body" meant the same thing.

I said, "The land is a body, and I am beginning to think it has something like speech."

"It is very eloquent," Elisabeth said.

We stood together and held the rails and I was glad the rails were white, a quiet colour that held all colours and did not fight with the promises or whatever eloquence existed in the body of the land: eloquence standing in the mountains or reclining in the slopes. I was glad our ship was blue and white, the colours of the water, and that our spirits were quiet, Elisabeth's and mine, not chattering or trying to translate what was being said or held by the ground in front of us. I thought of promises ricocheting all over the south: on signs, in mouths, on TV and radio and online. *Search no more*, promised the signs: *Here lies the end of your ravenous hunger in all its forms — just step right up, ladies and gentlemen.* We all knew the promises were fraudulent, but did we ever stop yearning?

I remembered what our pilot said as we flew over the Ungava Peninsula and Baffin Island: "There you are, folks...a whole lot of *nothing*."

But this wasn't nothing. It was something. The land was present, Elisabeth and I were present to it, and there was a silent interaction. Something in the encounter, an elemental force, had begun to exert an influence.

chapter eight

ANNIE'S DOLL

THERE WERE THINGS I did not know as I looked at the place we call the Northwest Passage but whose real name is known only to itself. Before I walked onshore, the land lay like a dreaming body whose dream emanated, brushed against me, and infused my body. Its eloquence and message remained quiet and mysterious as our ship approached. I couldn't believe we were really about to walk upon the blue, white, and gold vision itself. It seemed impossible but was not impossible. I'd been given the key to enter, to lie down and listen, to breathe its exhalations and hear it speak, and nobody does this without being changed.

But what I felt in the magical entrance to Pond Inlet was eclipsed, on our arrival, by a different reality. In fact, Europeans had named the body of water we now entered "Eclipse Sound," after a British whaling vessel hunting bowheads decades before Franklin's disappearance. "Eclipse" was a good word for what happened to my vision here. Things were not as they appeared, and there was more than one reality at play: layers superimposed on other layers.

The place names hint at this: we'd arrived in a land where nearly every landmark or settlement possesses two names. One name given by colonial explorers; another—older, indigenous—linked not to European, but to Inuit history. The British name "Pond Inlet" referred, not to ponds or lakes or any other real aspect of the place, but to an Englishman named John Pond who'd been the royal astronomer when British explorer John Ross named the area for the English in 1818. The Inuit name for Pond Inlet is Mittimatalik.

Ships don't often land at Pond Inlet: like most settlements in Canada's Far North, there are no dock facilities to accommodate them. Yet we soon saw that our vessel was not the only one visiting. Anchored in the waters near us loomed another ship: a large vessel whose occupants were visiting the inlet, as we were about to do—but for very different reasons.

We put on our rubber boots for a wet landing, which meant departing the ship in Zodiacs and wading toward the beach. I was excited at the thought of entering Canada after Greenland. I was my father. I was the immigrants who'd come to Canada before him. Here were the mountains, ice, and cold remoteness that had called to my dad since he was young. I'd come to Newfoundland passive and involuntary at age eight. But reaching Mittimatalik, I touched Canada for the first time with my own intent.

I felt a strange combination of newness and belonging: the North *was* the idea of Canada as perceived by the collective

unconscious of the world. I was a newcomer, yet had a passport and was allowed to stay. Approaching Pond Inlet became
a ceremony, like the rites by which a child is brought to a
spiritual path by parents and then chooses, at an age of reason,
to confirm this is where she belongs. In Newfoundland other
kids had sensed I was a stranger; I'd not known my grandparents or experienced rootedness. But on Mittimatalik's beach I
felt land's gravity reach and speak to me in no one's terms but
mine and its own.

Mountain, rock, and beach were substantial; there was
nothing vague about the gesture I perceived in their substance. It was clear to me I was undergoing a ritual created by
the ground itself, here in the Far North of a place some called
Canada, a place that had not been my birthplace but was offering now to accept me. This acceptance I had not expected to
feel and it moved me greatly: I felt the land's strength enclose
the energy of my own being as soon as I put my feet on it. I'd
never known a visceral connection with ground, but felt one
now. It was not a thing I'd imagined might happen, and I felt
wonderment.

But as we approached the beach I realized we would be
far from the only people interacting with the land. All along
the shore, crawling over the rocks and occupying the beach,
moved men and women in military gear: guns, badges, camouflage suits. The ship anchored near ours was an Arctic
war ship deployed by the Canadian Department of National
Defence. The Canadian military was visiting here in order
to carry out cold-weather tactical exercises as part of the federal government's latest push to assert sovereignty north of

the Arctic Circle. This was not just a cadet exercise like many I'd seen in the outports of Newfoundland, or in my children's schoolyards and gymnasia in a province where the army was perceived as one of few sure career choices for rural students. The troops covering the beaches of Mittimatalik were not cadets but soldiers, and with them strode Peter MacKay, then Canada's Minister of National Defence, clambering around the beach with an aura of great purpose.

The troops had overtaken a good part of the community, including the arena, where we were supposed to have played a friendly game of soccer with the people of the village. The building was now the soldiers' temporary dormitory, and our soccer game was not their kind of exercise. I'd been assigned as a cheerleader and was ready to wear a caustic green wig and a pink bikini over my woollens. Earlier, on board the ship, our players had chosen faux-Italian versions of their surnames and painted them on their shirts: Macgillverio, Martinello, and the like. Nathan Rogers had been taken aside and advised he'd gone too far and must not be spotted in a shirt proclaiming him as Fellatio. There'd been an all-night prayer vigil to ensure our team would lose respectably. We were looking forward to it.

Official word came through the grapevine, as we straggled up the beach, that the National Defence Minister would not be joining our team as star defenceman MacKaglio, nor would the soccer game go ahead at all, since his military personnel were busy conducting intensive naval exercises with the U.S. and Denmark, making much of Mittimatalik now out of bounds for civilians. MacKay did not have time to visit our ship, eat dinner with the captain, or take a virtual tour of the stunning new Geological Map of the Arctic with our geologist. Instead, we were now free to explore the non-militarized part of the community in disbanded form.

Some of our passengers chose to stay on the beach and take photographs of the younger soldiers—the sun lit their faces and they appeared proud and excited to be part of the government's military plan for the North.

"Have you been in the Far North before?" asked a passenger. "It must be exciting work."

"I admire what you're doing," said another. "We appreciate your hard work, the dedication of all the troops. May I shake your hand?"

I moved away from the uniforms and guns as quickly as I could. It had surprised me to see the beach occupied like this. I wanted to get away from it. I wanted to see Mittimatalik's daily life, its natural self, without any military ownership superimposed on it. But I realized that might be more difficult than I'd thought. The Canadian North has a long history of commercial, police, and military presence and, often, interference in the lives of the Inuit. I knew that from the 1920s through the 1950s and beyond, many Inuit had been coerced and even forcibly displaced from their traditional communities to satisfy a variety of outside interests—most infamously, perhaps, being forced to serve as "human flagpoles" in remote regions for the sake of Canadian Arctic sovereignty.

Southern governments appeared to share a view that it did not matter where Inuit people lived. To them, the North was all the same: featureless, frozen, and undifferentiated—a supposition born of ignorance and neglect that caused tragedy for untold displaced Inuit people, both in Canada and in the circumpolar regions of other countries. What seemed like an identical tract of land to white officials proved to Inuit to have unfamiliar contours and different animals or fish — sometimes no animals and no fish. Why did no one but the Inuit themselves understand that a person's homeland is sacred, sustaining, and irreplaceable?

As I retreated from the soldiers on the shore, I felt the line dissolve between what we call history and the present: the line between then and now impressed itself on me as an illusory boundary, like national borders and measurements of time. Everything about this gateway to the Northwest Passage, including its military occupants, spoke of a present moment firmly connected not just to the land's own intrinsic life, but to a strikingly evident geopolitical past and future.

STRUCTURES HERE WERE very different from houses and businesses in Greenland. Here stood no red, yellow, or green houses flanked by daisies or purple cottonweed. There was no café with a sign offering smoked seal or caribou with juniper berries. Pond Inlet's houses were either unpainted or shaded in muted greys and greens. Building this far above the treeline came at exorbitant cost, as it did in Greenland. But these structures held none of the aesthetic cheerfulness of the Greenlandic houses we'd sketched or painted or photographed. They were like the government-issued prefab units I'd seen when filming documentary work and teaching in Shetshatshiu, Labrador. This is the case in much of Canada's

North: the Nunavut government's 2010 Housing Needs Survey found forty-nine percent of homes in the territory to be substandard—often overcrowded and in need of major repair. The difference in atmosphere between the social conditions here and in Greenland was immediately apparent, and passengers talked about it, especially those who weren't Canadian and had little knowledge of how Canadian indigenous people's lives have been reshaped by government policy issuing from the urban south.

"Why are the houses so derelict?" asked Mary, an American.

As I walked the grey road I saw, ahead, an Inuk with a handmade doll. It was a mother doll in an embroidered, fur-edged amauti with a child doll in the hood, and it was for sale. In Greenland we'd meandered uphill and down, past curtained dwellings and outbuildings, and we did the same here.

I remembered summers in Newfoundland when I'd been a person living in a town others visit. On Water Street in St. John's, and on a ferry from Woody Point to Norris Point, Americans had wanted to take photographs of a Newfoundland woman with her red-haired child. "Oh, she looks just like Anne of Green Gables! Do you mind if we take your photo to show our friends back in Pennsylvania that we met little Canadian Annie?"

"Go ahead."

The Woody Point ferryman had played Newfoundland jigs: visitors wanted fiddles and accordions. He made detours for the visitors so the trip, which normally took fifteen minutes to ferry locals to work or the doctor or the store, glittered with dolphin pods and shimmering mackerel and the history of an abandoned settlement. It could cut into the local people's day by an hour and a half.

When I was living near Brigus, I took care to go into the village only when the blueberry festival tents weren't up and the horse and cart rides were finished and Meg Ryan and Daniel Radcliffe had stopped hanging incognito around the house with the sign that said *Esther's Homemade Bread*, and one autumn day I visited Brigus Public Library and heard:

"I'm elated they're gone."

"Tell me about it. Traipsing six inches in front of your window, poking their noses right through your curtains and then doing it again backwards."

"I'm asphyxiated with it."

"'Asphyxiated' is the right word, Madeleine. You hit the nail on the head there. I don't care if I never set eyes on another stranger as long as I draw breath. And me with two sons who can't afford to live in their own hometown because the tourists don't want to see trailer homes in any of our fields. I'd like to wrap a few trailer homes around their necks and see how they like that."

As an outsider myself I'd felt interest and amusement as I listened, but here in Pond Inlet, as I watched everyone pass by the woman and her handmade doll, I wondered how she felt.

By the time I reached her, I was surprised that still no one had bought her doll. Maybe someone had promised to pay on the way back down to the ship.

"Has anyone said they'll buy your doll?"

She shook her head.

"How much is it?"

"A hundred dollars."

I knew a hundred dollars was a good price for the doll. Someone coming up behind me would buy it, one of the Americans, maybe, who'd know they couldn't get such a doll anywhere else on earth. I continued uphill, leaving the maker behind. She had a little girl with her. I wanted time to walk alone and think about how I was feeling in this first stop on the Northwest Passage. How unsettling that the military entourage of the Minister of National Defence should be here just as we arrived. It seemed an unlikely coincidence, yet I knew the Prime Minister himself now made an Arctic trip yearly, making a point of creating media buzz around his presence and his intention to build on past Canadian governments' use of northern settlements as markers of ownership. These trips were signals to other countries: signals that Canada planned to stake aggressive claim to its Far Northern shores and all the sapphires, oil, and other geological riches they contained, especially now that ancient barriers of ice were melting.

I walked to the Co-op store. Outside on its wooden rails someone had scrawled the kind of message my teen daughter had graffitied in her school bus shelter in Newfoundland:

I'm tired of
this town
I wish I
can go some
where

In the lobby a young mother hunkered down at the bub-
blegum machine, her baby in her amauti and her older son
clutching his fireman doll and deciding between Dubble Bub-
ble and Rascals fruit chews. She wore sunglasses and until I
took her photo like the tourists in Newfoundland had taken
mine, I didn't notice her bruises.

Inside stood shelves of corned beef and baked beans, tins
of ravioli, acrylic yarn and plastic flashlights and white bread,
all at exorbitant prices. A fridge bore green peppers and iceberg lettuces strangled in plastic. I saw the Kit Kats and Mars
Bars, chips and sodas I'd seen in convenience stores in southern towns where the mills had shut and no one had registered
children for kindergarten in a long time. Celery and wieners
sat criminally priced and way past their best-before dates. A
bulletin board bore notice that next month a dentist would fill
cavities, fit dentures, and treat mouth diseases. I knew a nurse
who'd come here to treat tuberculosis, a disease my mother
nearly died of in England when she was young, but which my
world now considered a thing of the past.

But my reference points didn't belong here. Anything I
might assume about life in the North was based on knowledge
from a different way of being. It was easy enough for me to see
a threadbare version of southern cultural coordinates: a can of
condensed milk at seven dollars, a drafty bungalow priced far
out of reach. But this wasn't the whole picture.

I thought of fish and wild meat in rural Newfoundland and
how it represented all that might be invisible about a place to
a person who was just passing through. There were outports
in my province where a visitor might look in the convenience

stores and wonder how anyone there ever got a decent bite to eat. They might go to a restaurant around the bay and think Newfoundlanders lived on corn dogs and deep fried mozza sticks and in some cases they might be right. Food sovereignty has been and is becoming a crisis in the rural places of the western world: here in Mittimatalik just as in Rocky Harbour, Newfoundland, and Green Bay, Wisconsin and places all over the world, food crimes are being committed by multinational producers and distributors, by governments, shopkeepers, and educators — some of it unconscious, but much of it a direct result of corporate greed and a collective cultural somnambulism. Yet underneath the corporate food system in small-town Newfoundland, and more so in the Canadian North, remains a connection to real food from local land and water. I remembered how in Greenland Aaju Peter had rejected the commercialization of wild food. I sensed in her view an unease I shared, at how harvesting and sharing wild, nutritious food has become imperilled by economic forces sweeping the globe.

In Newfoundland I'd known an old woman who ran an outport post office from her house. She ate herring and partridgeberries and seabirds whose local names are found only in Newfoundland's own dictionary. But this was in the 1980s, and the next generation wouldn't even look at wild food. I wondered if such a transition was afoot in Mittimatalik.

In Innu communities in Labrador I'd seen that a lot depended on whether people were holed up in government housing or out on the land. I visited houses then saw tents on the land and knew these were two worlds. I listened to grandfathers who kept old ways, then heard their adult sons and daughters who lived in a hybrid world — between old, wild wisdom with its hardship, and a new simulation of southern suburbia with electric heat and factory bread, disorientation and emptiness. Children went to school wearing Disney Pocahontas backpacks.

Now, at the top of the hill, a few passengers gathered around Aaju, asking questions about the difference between Pond Inlet and the villages we had seen in Greenland. Aaju was visibly relieved to be back in the north of Canada, and this puzzled some of the passengers, who'd seen the Greenlandic people as more prosperous than the Inuit here.

"Why," they asked her, "did you choose to live in the Canadian North, when you already had a homeland that seems so much more economically and socially stable?"

"I could never leave Nunavut," Aaju said. "I lived as a Greenlandic woman for years, then as a Canadian Inuk woman, and I would never go back."

"Why?"

"I can never leave Nunavut after learning their teachings."

"What teachings?"

"People here relate to people, and not to titles, degrees, or importance."

"But what about the economy?" asked Yvonne, an American. We'd all seen the Greenlandic butcher shop, with its sparkling tubs of fresh wild seal, reindeer, halibut, and caplin. "Here in Pond Inlet we see no sale of wild meat or fish."

"That's because in Greenland, unlike here, hunters and fishermen sell their catch," Aaju said. "It is part of a cash economy. They are allowed to sell it."

Everyone nodded as if this were a great idea. We understood licenses that allowed people to exchange goods. We
liked quality control and free market prices based on supply
and demand. Wouldn't something like that be better here in
Pond Inlet than a not-so-super market mirroring others in
Canada's Far North—frozen, breaded chicken at ten times
the cost of buying it in Etobicoke? For a hundred bucks you
had yourself a full-meal deal just like in the movies, except it
was freezer-burnt and you had to thaw it yourself. Surely the
Kalaalimineerniarfik fish markets in Ilulissat and other Greenlandic villages were an improvement?

"Yes," Aaju said, "Greenland towns have fresh markets
where fishermen and hunters get a fair price for their wild
catches. But Inuit people in Canada do not sell their catch.
They share it."

ON MY WAY back down to Pond Inlet's beach I straggled
behind and saw the Inuk woman still standing on the road
with her little girl and handmade doll.

"No one bought your doll?"

She shook her head again.

"Can I buy it?"

She handed it to me. It was heavier than I thought it would
be. Under the grass-green amauti flared a little cotton dress
scattered with roses and finished with a hand-stitched hem.
A strand of glass beads, tinted the turquoise, gold, and silver
of the waters we'd just sailed, decorated the coat's extravagant tail; another hung from the gathered waist. The coat was

embroidered, the mittens and boots sewn of felt and leather edged with seal, bear, and fox fur. Snug in the hood nestled the baby doll, her hair of black wool bound with a fine-cut rawhide string. I gave the maker the hundred dollars. She'd signed the soles of the doll's boots — the left, in Inuktitut syllabary; the right, *Annie Qillaq Pewqtoqlook*. I felt very forlorn about buying the doll.

As we waited on the beach for the Zodiacs to take us back to the ship, I saw that Nathan Rogers had collected a gaggle of teenage Inuit girls; they stared, rapt, at his tongue piercing as they bit their chipped blue nail polish, agog at the unearthly sound he was making. We'd heard Inuit throat-singing in the community, but now Nathan was Mongolian throat-singing, a demented hurdy-gurdy clamouring to escape his solar plexus. The setting sun made his tongue stud glitter as the noise curled across the beach, and the girls looked as if they believed the sound might turn into some mythical animal and change their lives forever. They were astonished and afraid, and Nathan enjoyed this very much, throwing his head back and letting the crazy sound gather force and curl out again. He was a sorcerer and the girls had been waiting for a sorcerer, and they were especially astounded when he told them that what he was doing was first cousin to the very throat-singing they themselves, their mothers, aunts, and grandmothers knew.

"Teach us!"

He started on a couple of rudiments but we had to go. The girls hated to see him leave, but he said they could do it without him. "Just practice."

"How long?"

"Thousands of hours."

"Thousands!"

"But you can do it. You just have to get the basics then it's totally up to you and how much you practice. If you practice like I practice you'll be able to do it just as well, I promise."

"But how are we gonna get the basics?"

"You can learn it the same place I did."

"Where?"

"YouTube."

chapter nine

EMILY CARR'S MILK BILL

THAT EVENING WE left Pond Inlet to sail for Dundas Harbour. In the ship's dining room I noticed a wiry little woman called Georgie with whom I'd not yet spoken. How had I not noticed her before? With her unruly hair and electric intensity, she appeared to me as Amelia Earhart might have looked had she lived another twenty years. At a table for two she sat alone, tearing into a fluffy bun.

"May I?" I touched the empty chair.

"By all means!"

"What's on the menu?"

"Risotto, carrot ginger soup."

"Nice. And look. I don't usually eat dessert"—this was becoming a lie—"but tonight they have some kind of chocolate bomb with sorbet." I wrote this down in my little notebook.

"You're a writer?"

"Yes."

"I've seen you sketching, too. You're taking Sheena's art workshops, aren't you?"

"I'm trying."

"When I was twenty-one," Georgie said, "my dad used to deliver milk to Emily Carr."

"Emily *Carr*?"

I'd read *The Book of Small*, Carr's idiosyncratic account of being a child in B.C. at the end of the 1800s: wooden bathtubs in the living room, noisy barn sparrows, childish wonders that hit you like a stomach ache or tickled your thinking until you were driven half mad. I'd seen reproductions of Carr's paintings of the magnificent totem poles around Haida Gwaii, and also of the paintings she made after her contact with the Group of Seven's Lawren Harris, who advised her to leave off interpreting aboriginal culture and concentrate on expressing her own vision directly. I remembered feeling, even while looking at a tiny reproduction of one of her trees, the weight of that tree as entity, as living agent with power and intent.

"Emily Carr, yes. He was her milkman."

"Her milkman!"

One of the differences between my life as a child in England and as an immigrant in Canada had been the absence, in Canada, of milkmen. According to friends, I'd narrowly missed the milkman's demise in Newfoundland. I remember being extremely disappointed at the discovery of supermarket homogenized milk, which meant you did not get glass bottles delivered, clinking on your doorstep, or peel their foil tops to reveal a thick layer of pure cream you could beg your mother to let you lick from a saucer like a cat.

"Yes. My dad was Emily Carr's milkman. And she couldn't pay her milk bill."

I balanced an exquisite portion of risotto on the end of my fork. Risotto is a dish I've revered since my first taste. I've seen it made on television and have looked it up on YouTube, and have eaten perfect examples in good restaurants or at friends' houses, but only five or six times. For me it's a rare delicacy, and I've never felt brave enough to make it. My daughter Juliette made it for me when she was twelve. She followed a heritage recipe to create a lemon version that was all density yet light as a cloud — ethereal and tantalizing comfort food, somehow inaccessible even while you're eating it.

"Emily Carr couldn't pay her milk bill?"

"My father came home and told my mother, 'Emily Carr wants to know can she pay with a painting, or would you rather wait 'til she has the money.'"

It wasn't hard to imagine my own husband coming home and saying something like that to me. He gets up on people's roofs and cleans the chimneys and sometimes the flashing needs to be mended or there are bricks loose, and he gives people the diagnosis. He doesn't necessarily tell them everything. Years ago, as he was pushing and pulling his brush to clean soot from a famous Quebec singer's chimney, which had a bend in it, the brush broke in the bend, where he says it remains. Once he was on a roof, people remembered they also needed pianos lowered down fire escapes, or valves replaced on propane tanks, and while he was at it there were beams half-eaten by ants. He came home with lots of payments that weren't money: jam, haircuts, hindquarters from the family pig. Once, for moving a freezer out of a man's basement, he came home with two paintings by Paul Parsons, an artist who rode, dressed in smart suits and ties from the Salvation Army, on a bike the local Tim Hortons had given him from its cache of roll-up-the-rim prizes as a sort of community recognition of his status as artist of the streets.

I'd read an essay by Daniel Francis on Emily Carr and knew she had waxed and waned in her painting practice throughout her life. I knew she'd given up painting for years and had managed to stay afloat by opening a boarding house. I imagined Emily Carr making toast and jam, baked beans and cake for her boarders while hoarding a stash of her master-works in the attic — to be later discovered by National Gallery of Canada director Eric Brown, mercifully in time for her to resume a second act as a painter of her more personal visions. But she spent years not painting, looking after boarders, mak-ing their beds and their tea, and doing untold loads of laundry in an old wringer-washer.

"And what did your mother say?" I asked the daughter of Emily Carr's milkman.

"She said, 'Wait 'til she has the money.'"

Georgie gave me the rueful look that means see how awful family stories can be. It meant what wouldn't Georgie give now for that painting by Emily Carr, bartered for the daily milk. And it meant see how we're fools, and how we must for-give our fathers and sometimes our mothers for viewing life trapped in a prism of practicality and function. But it was also fun to dwell on this story of regret and imagine the painting that might have been Georgie's had the chance not been lost.

"The milk at that time," said Georgie, "was fifteen cents a pint."

The sorbet arrived. I grew up eating great piles of minced moose my dad hunted and Savoy cabbage he grew in his garden and Yorkshire pudding filled with puddles of gravy my mother slaved over in the kitchen, and with that kind of dinner who needed pudding? But our ship's dessert chef had my number. He somehow knew blackberries had grown on the brambles around my dad's allotment when I was a child, and that I had a blackberry-stained mouth until I was eight. He'd made blackberry sorbet, and as Georgie and I ate it off pretty spoons I pondered the milk at fifteen cents a pint that Emily Carr had not been able to afford.

I remembered the day it dawned on me that my first husband had no intention of earning a cent but had ensconced himself in my tiny apartment as a sort of resident writer of unpublished radio plays. My own writing — theatre reviews and stories in local literary journals — earned enough to scrape up rent and groceries for one. He decided he'd start going to a church where they spoke in tongues and had a food bank, and on Sundays he brought home packets of ground beef. We had a fire escape three floors up, and I decided since it was so close to the heavens I'd sit on it and have a celestial rant. Eight months pregnant, I beseeched the heavens to get money up there so I could go downstairs and buy a bloody eggplant. That husband loathed eggplants. He looked at the sight of an eggplant as some sort of personal affront.

I was furious with my own stupidity. Why hadn't it registered that before marrying me — in his thirties — he'd lived in a tiny room upstairs at his mother's house around the bay? Granted, that room had been stuffed with stolen Penguin paperbacks, their orange spines proudly arranged in alphabetical order by author. I'd been hoodwinked by those Penguins and by that lilac tree grazing his window, its hundred-year-old branches laden with fragrant blooms. I meant to sit on our fire escape until by some divine intervention there appeared money to go down to Lar's Fruit Mart.

I bellyached until I heard someone run up the stairs. That was a set of stairs I'll never forget: three storeys of winding ascent, brutal for a pregnant woman with no vegetables in her. I knew our poverty was of my own making but still, couldn't a scrap of light from that youthful hope I'd once known have stopped me in time from getting into this predicament? Then: Who was that on the stairs? All the way up, knocking on our door... I got off my perch and found one of the men from the tongues-speaking ground beef church standing there and clutching a hundred dollar bill.

"The Lord," he gasped (he was old for our stairs), "told me to come here and give you this."

"I was praying," he said, "and God told me to stop right there and come up here and give you this money."

He wiped his face and started back downstairs, and I took the money and bought grapes, cheese, and bread and some very good salami. I still remember the cracked peppercorns in the hard, transparent salami slices, and I think there might have been a bottle of wine to cap off the extravagance.

So I could see Emily Carr's pantry, her house, her cats, and her Joseph's Coat plant with its maroon leaves, drinking sunlight from a tiny window. I saw her bottle of milk with its lid winking in the light. She would have foregone the milk, I'm nearly sure, were it not that she'd promised a saucer of it to one of her beloved cats.

"Father had every colour of cat," she'd written in *The Book of Small*. "He took fresh milk in a bottle from home every morning to them; he said a diet of straight rat was not healthy for cats."

This, I thought, was the kind of thing you never forgot, not even if you grew to be ninety, if your father had taught it to you as a child.

That night I leaned against the deck rails watching the white wake and thinking about Georgie's account of Emily Carr's milk bill. It was a forlorn tale, but maybe living with the story enlarged it: instead of losing the chance to own a single painting by a woman of genius, Georgie somehow gained Emily Carr's entire output. In the attic of her own mind, Georgie could imagine whichever Emily Carr painting she might *nearly* have owned, rendering ambiguous and perhaps less tragic the steadfast practicality of a mother who put up with no nonsense. Maybe practicality had unexpected benefits, I thought. Maybe it was okay, once in a while, to know your coordinates, to pinpoint exactly where you stood.

On the ship's port side was pinned a map of Greenland and Canada on which someone daily penciled our progress. The line snaked now from Kangerlussuaq in southern Greenland, up the white coast through Sisimiut, Ilulissat, Karrat Fjord, and Upernavik, across Baffin Bay to Pond Inlet. Usually someone more knowledgeable than I wielded the pencil: one of the geologists, or one of our archaeologist's more avid students. But this time I took my own pencil stub, normally used to sketch bones and flora and undulating hills, and scrawled our latest progress: up the narrow channel between Baffin and Bylot Islands, and north across Lancaster Sound.

chapter ten

GEOLOGY

BY MORNING WE were approaching Dundas Harbour on Devon Island's southern shore. I sat in the dining room with my coffee, ignoring the ripple of excitement passing through the air as passengers listened to something about rocks on the loudspeaker.

Marc St-Onge was forever enthusing about some looming outcrop of this or that rock, calling all passengers to see things from a plate tectonic point of view. At the start of our journey he'd distributed a geo-briefing book: we'd study granitic orthogneiss and intruding granite plutons, and look at the way things were in northeastern North America before Paleocene rifting sixty million years ago.

I don't think so . . . I'd inched farther from Marc's nucleus of instruction.

Before this voyage I'd fled rooms where people sat in front of documentaries in which David Suzuki and his team of animators tried to make continents and mountains appear to lurch and collide and cause untold drama and disruption. I had nothing but respect for the man when he was talking about things that actually move, but the thought of listening to five minutes of a geological lecture filled me with ennui, no matter how internationally acclaimed the professor.

Rarely, then, could an announcement by our geologist lure me from the dining room's Lurpak butter, even as others clambered on deck to see the Rae Craton or to scan rocks for narwhal, which some say is the real animal on which we've built our idea of the unicorn. I didn't go around with my camera ready, and had more interest in things I might encounter without going out of my way than for curiosities — even ones that actually moved — requiring effort or diversion. I liked to think this was not laziness but an extension of my habit of seeing. I liked to observe some detail about a person, something about the room, the land, or the sky, without hearing an announcement or abandoning my croissant for the tail-end of some glorious breaching of a whale that wasn't my sight to see. I felt that if a narwhal or other astonishing creature wanted to reveal something to me, it would do so when we were both ready.

So as I tackled a perfectly poached egg on thin Russian toast, I did not rise as our geologist announced we should go on deck immediately to see a magnificent display of nonconforming rocks on the port side. I stayed until the room was cleared but for a man administering something onto his food from a mysterious vial. The nonconforming rocks, visible through the windows, appeared to be a perfectly normal-looking ribbon of blue hills in the distance, each section conforming very nicely with the next in a continuous, fluid line. What *were* nonconforming rocks, anyway? They must be rocks that behaved in a way different from the rocks surrounding them, jiving when the others waltzed, partying as the rest studied for exams. They wore unconventional mantles and sprouted impossible lichen, and at night, as other rocks slept, the nonconforming rocks planned renegade activities. This took place over eons, visible only to those with deep vision who could assemble four-dimensional jigsaw puzzles of minuscule shards.

Nonconforming rocks were nectar for our geologist and his disciples, and no doubt my truancy would come back to haunt me. But I was attracted to nonconforming events in moments passing now, in front of me, in the atmosphere and personalities on the ship: I was interested when the man who remained with his mysterious vial said, "I am interested in mustard."

"Mustard?"

"People are not nearly as interested in mustard as they should be."

"Aren't they?"

"Mustard is a natural antimicrobial agent. The world is crying out for it. In the next century do you know what farmers will be doing? They will put mustard into the soil before they plant their crops, and the caustic powers of the mustard will kill harmful microbes. Then, when the natural caustic gases have dispersed, the farmers will be able to plant their crops with no worries, no danger at all, from the microbes which now infest their farmland."

I hadn't noticed, but I noticed now, that Mr. Mustard's

jacket bore a beautifully stitched insignia, *Mustard 21 Canada Inc.*, embroidered within fronds of a golden plant. He raised his vial and offered me its contents: a special preparation for spicing up one's shipboard meal. I was interested in this. I found it very nonconforming.

Do you sleep in the park? I wanted to ask him. *Or in a hole in the road?*

Was I in the Northwest Passage with Mean Mr. Mustard himself, en route to Coppermine from Abbey Road?

I could imagine a man like Mr. Mustard summoning his associates and collectively pouring powder into farmers' soil. The tune of a song and vials of golden powder affected me in ways geological facts did not. It escaped me that everything my family and I *were* in this world had come about because seams of coal lay under the ground where we were born. I had not taken in the importance of the new circumpolar Arctic geological map our geologist and his colleagues had completed in time for the International Polar Year. Had I even understood that Samuel Hearne's eighteenth-century traipse toward our destination of Kugluktuk, or Coppermine, had aimed to discern whether minerals, especially copper, could be commercially mined? The larger colonial push to get ships through the Northwest Passage beyond Hearne's time had lunged for India's sapphires, rubies, and gold, all products of geology. The moon and stars, of which I was so fond, were all rock, and if I took everything I ever saw, used, thought of, or exchanged with others, I'd see it had come from ground: ground was the seemingly inert, dense thing from which all liveliness and light emerged. But I hadn't begun to see this, drunk on the products and effects of ground and ignorant of their cause. I was seduced by word, culture, idea — not imagining these might be mere side-effects emanating from the ground of their origin.

IF THE EARTH's geological speech was beginning to get through to other passengers, Nathan Rogers had begun reminding me of layers of being I'd shared with no one. Through Paris and Naples, San Francisco and Albuquerque, I'd travelled alone. I'd walked Montmartre and haggled with tomato sellers in alleys off Spaccanapoli, feeling lonely but regarding that as the price you had to pay for the freedom of meandering unhitched to someone else's agenda.

In France I ended up having a cockroach slipped in my *chocolat chaud* by a waitress whose boyfriend, an Italian jazz pianist named Mario, had taken to loitering under the geraniums hanging from the balcony of my cheap hotel. In Naples I'd escaped falling chairs and pianos and an Egyptian with a gold tooth by stealing enough bread, sausage and spinach to let me hide out in my hotel basement before escaping on the midnight train. In New Mexico I'd outstayed my welcome at a hostel on Route 66 and roomed in an adobe house with itinerants who sold their plasma for food stamps and ate nothing but porridge until one of their mothers sent a box of peanut butter, tuna, and Oreos from New Jersey. A bench near Golden Gate Bridge was where I learned, unfolding the *San Francisco Chronicle* the day after Valentine's in 1982, that the oil rig Ocean Ranger had sunk off the shore of the land I'd left behind, killing eighty-four Newfoundlanders, and I walked Haight-Ashbury holding a tear-soaked avocado sandwich.

Somehow none of these things taught me a person can never really know the world alone. In later travels with others, even in my marriages and as a mother, I'd strived to keep an envelope of solitude around myself. I liked having a pocket of air around my body that no one could inhabit, to make room for my thoughts, or for pools of emptiness in which ideas might be born.

The Northwest Passage would have seemed a perfect place to continue this practice: horizons stretching into distance, bodies of water that froze, crashed, and shifted, then melted but froze again. On the middle deck I often stood alone — the others hung out elsewhere to lounge, talk, and scan the sea for narwhals, and I had no idea where the party was. I enacted my own name — Winter — and didn't believe I needed a friend.

At night in the tiny library I continued drawing Elisabeth's thirty-year-old woollen undergarment, taking care to mark its sepia colours and delicate lines in the sketchbook Sheena McGoogan had encouraged me to keep. I loved Elisabeth and Sheena in my own way, a winterish way, a kind of respectful enjoyment, from a comfortable distance, of others who shared a quiet soul and a love for stories. When I tired of sketching I crocheted my skein of hand-dyed yarn into warm headgear, and I read or watched the blue Arctic night out the portholes as the ship carried us along in its sweet rocking. I was self-contained and I suppose you could have called me standoffish, as there was nothing better I liked to do than stand off at the edge of everything.

But Nathan was having none of that. I realized as we began navigating Lancaster Sound that each time I reached the brink of deepest aloneness he'd pop out of some doorway or from behind boulders in his yellow jacket with his look of...I could only call it complicity. We were eleven years old. We were twelve. We were the age I'd been when the first hint of something tantalizing and immaterial made itself known to me, glinting from beyond the ordinary world with which grownups seemed so contented.

Here he comes, I thought, each time he broke in, and with each of those times I felt the solitude matter less, the friendship more.

Nathan was a walking, talking, songwriting, sword-bearing soul on a hero's quest, and he was kind to me. Not only had he refrained from hoisting my concertina overboard, he'd offered to accompany me when I sang "Lady Franklin's Lament" one night in the forward lounge.

"You want me to back you up on the guitar?"

"But my concertina's...it's a battered old thing, made in Germany fifty years ago." It was the model sold for pennies to every Irish household that wanted a ship's piano on the mantelpiece.

"So?"

"It's sort of...developed its own voice."

"Fine by me."

"But it's out of tune with every other instrument on the planet."

"I'm not one little bit worried about that. If you want me to accompany you I'll be fine. Trust me."

Somehow Nathan tuned his guitar perfectly to my demented squeezebox, though to do this he had to be more than a professional; he had to be a magician.

At night in the main lounge he sang story ballads from folk traditions from all over the world, compositions of his own that drew from those traditions or drew from something else entirely that was his alone, and the songs of his father, Stan Rogers — songs passengers knew by heart like the iconic "Northwest Passage." When Nathan sang Stan's songs his whole being changed, and it struck me that singing them was how he'd come to know his father since his death. He was a reed through which the songs of his lost father blew. Was it a strain to share knowledge of your father with audiences who knew the songs and claimed the man as partly theirs? Here in the Northwest Passage, singing "The Northwest Passage," Nathan inhabited a legend within a legend, and I wondered how that felt.

"My father's death," he told me, "was not an accident."

He recounted the events that must have been told to him many times over the years: Air Canada flight 797 filling with smoke on the tarmac and then, before passengers could exit, becoming engulfed in flash flames. It happened, Nathan said, because of woefully inadequate safety mechanisms, and the disaster led to massive improvements in air travel worldwide.

I remembered seeing him lift Motoko, the Japanese passenger who'd fractured her foot, up staircases onto the ship, gathering her in his arms as his father must have held the aircraft passengers he saved. There was no doubt in my mind that Nathan carried more than the songs of his father. He carried a burden of images and stories that belonged to all people to whom his father meant so much—and he had to be content with sharing those memories graciously with strangers.

In the lounge one night Nathan sang a song called "Dark Eyed Molly," written by Glasgow's Archie Fisher—a song his father had also sung. The first time Nathan sang it I didn't understand the depth of what I felt. Our historian, Ken McGoogan, gave an involuntary cry at the end. That song contained such sorrow and beauty: Nathan's, Archie Fisher's, Ken's, and mine, as well as some forlornness that perhaps belonged to the ship, and I had to leave the room for my comfort zone, the library, where I could unwind handspun wool and work with my hands and be alone. It was becoming apparent to me that geologists were not the only ones on board beginning to see how space, rock, and time form pressurized material that can manifest in surprising outcrops, breaking through ground we think we see and know.

But Nathan followed with his guitar.

"Would you like a private concert?"

He didn't wait for my answer. In a little armchair he sat, and began singing.

As my first husband lay dying in the hospital, my friend Ed Kavanagh offered to come to my house and play for me. He brought his Celtic harp, which, though small, filled the tiny room where I lay on the couch, depleted by the strain of weeks and years with someone ill in the house. I'd heard of therapeutic music for people who are sick or weary, but hadn't experienced it. The harp music filled the house, waves of a golden ocean, and the waves entered my body and lent me their energy in a way I could not have expected. Ed played a whole afternoon, without talk or fanfare, and when done he quietly picked up the harp and left me alone with ebbing ripples of pure beauty.

For Nathan's private concert I had no dying husband, no reason why I deserved the gift other than an offering of friendship, and this hadn't happened to me before. Somehow everything I'd learned about life pointed to an idea that to receive something you had to earn it. I'd never thought of myself as a tree, a graceful being visited by songbird, starlight, and rain, and which people love for itself, not for what it does or how smart it is, or how indispensable. I was used to making myself indispensable in one arena or another, but Nathan's song turned me into that tree.

He knew I loved "Dark Eyed Molly." It was the first of many times he'd sing it for me on the voyage, and every time he did I could hardly believe I was allowed to hear it again.

chapter eleven

DUNDAS HARBOUR

OUR OFFICIAL REASON for entering Dundas Harbour was to visit the ruins of an RCMP outpost, stationed in 1923 — and operated intermittently until its abandonment in 1951 — as part of the Canadian government's fight to resist other nations' claims to the Arctic archipelago. Britain had turned the territory over to Canada in 1880; but with no one actually occupying the place, Canada knew its professed ownership to be fragile and even merely symbolic. The RCMP post at Dundas Harbour was part of a larger project, begun in 1922, that saw detachments spring up throughout the very part of the High Arctic our journey was now entering.

We'd see a bit of Canadian police history; plenty of artifacts remained on the tundra for us to look at. But we had to walk there, and we each had such different perceptions of what to expect that we might have been on separate journeys. Marc St-Onge was excited because Dundas Harbour possessed one of the most wondrous unconformities in the world: a visible, rock-defined time-gap as thrilling to Marc and his followers as a vision from Dr. Who's TARDIS or Madeleine L'Engle or Albert Einstein might be to those captivated by mysteries of time. While I glazed over at the mention of continental margin sequences, Marc and those passengers whose imaginations he'd ignited were thrilled. I was still mulling over the word "unconformities" and was intrigued by terms like "crystalline basement," but what they conjured in my mind had nothing to do with geology. Unconformities might as well have been asymmetrical entities with hair that doubled as sensitive antennae, bedecked with dewdrops that saw through opaque matter. A crystalline basement might be made of amethyst; not ordinary geological amethyst, but an enhanced version, with hidden blue flames through which one approached the palace of Kubla Khan.

But then Marc said something that captivated me. Quoting Scottish geologist James Hutton, he stood on a bed of stones and proclaimed, "'The present is the key to the past' on a global scale."

I saw and felt this at Dundas Harbour: not necessarily in the rock, but in the Icelandic poppies, whose old, brown stems from previous years curled around their new stems. I saw it in the ancient roots of ground-hugging shrubs, silvered with age yet possessed of a current life, now, deep in their centres. It was in the muskox bones and skulls that lay where their owners had died on the grasses, and it was in the forlorn ruins of the RCMP quarters down the hill, where star grasses and poppies sprang, living, between the cracks of buildings that sagged with palpable remnants of tragedy. I didn't want to go down to the buildings but everyone else was headed there, and we'd been warned, by the gunbearers, to be sure to stay together.

Behind me came the bird people. I hated getting caught in the middle of their discussions about the powers of the massive cameras slung around their necks.

I overheard, "How many megabytes is your small raw?"

"Yesterday"—did I imagine the respondent cast me a mocking glance?—"I had a problem and the first thing I had to do was *cut off* my small raw."

I'd had a lover who lived in a house of birders, and I knew they risked perilous cliffs, frostbite, and alienation from all human warmth to glimpse what they called "a good bird." I'd liked that lover—except for the time I found some woman's giant underpants in his bed and he tried to persuade me they were mine—but I was only a diversion while his own good bird was away at university. So I'd escaped birdhouse life, but knew these passengers were not in Dundas Harbour for geological unconformities or wrinkles in time, nor for the desolate remnants of an abandoned RCMP station. They wanted fulmars, little brown cranes, and the ever-elusive red-throated loon.

To me any bird was a good bird. A pigeon, with its oil-slick throat and eyes the brown of beer bottles in the sun, was an excellent bird. So were the Polish chickens I'd owned, with their mops of crazy headgear; I'd fed my children their green eggs with ham. I loved a boyhood story my dad had told me about how his paper route took him through English birdsong that he called the "dawn chorus." I'd met a boreal owl in the woods and had put him in my novel. A pair of northern flickers with blood-red drops on their heads had consoled me, cooing under my bedroom window after my first husband's death. The bird whose song owns my heart is a hermit thrush, and winnowing snipe have never stopped haunting me. I loved birds, but they were free to come near or mind their own business. I would not pursue them with a *raw*, big or small, and I didn't want to cross them off any list or proclaim some more desirable than others.

The birders passed me on their trek to the abandoned RCMP station and I straggled far behind, kneeling to look at grass and bones and the strange nodding campion flower that looked, in bud, like a mauve paper lantern. But Aaju Peter, walking with her gun, admonished me.

"You have to keep going. You're not supposed to walk behind the gunbearer. It's very important."

So I climbed down to the ruins, where a rusted sewing machine occupied an open sill, paused to make the next stitch. A table bore canisters with remnants of food and drink, and a tiny graveyard cradled the remains of Constables Victor Maisonneuve, who killed himself in 1926, and William Stephens, who died the following year in a hunting accident, as well as the remains of a mysterious child. The isolation must have been unbearable for those officers, alone and subjected to perpetual darkness from November to February. Devon Island, on whose southern shore Dundas Harbour is situated, is the biggest uninhabited island on earth. But it was not just the ghosts of Maisonneuve and Stephens that I felt.

Dundas Harbour was more than simply a police outpost:

economic conditions in the 1930s meant Canada needed to look for a cheaper way to occupy the High Arctic. It also feared that simply planting a few police constables did not really constitute occupation of the land according to international law. What you needed was a legitimate, settled population. In his paper "Out in the Cold: The Legacy of Canada's Inuit Relocation Experiment in the High Arctic," cultural historian Alan Marcus explains how in 1934 the Department of the Interior launched an experiment, implemented by the Hudson's Bay Company, relocating ten Inuit families from Cape Dorset, Pangnirtung, and Pond Inlet to Dundas Harbour.

The government of the 1930s publicly said the same things it would say during later incarnations of this kind of resettlement in the 1950s, when it would send hundreds of Inuit families far from their homes to occupy the High Arctic in accordance with sovereignty concerns. It promised the Inuit better hunting and fishing farther north, though it made no wildlife studies to support the claims, which turned out to be untrue: many Inuit starved. In reality, it appeared that the government's claim of better hunting masked another motive. Alan Marcus quotes a 1935 government document that confesses the political reasons for the displacement of Inuit families to Dundas Harbour:

> In addition to the placing of the Eskimos in new regions where game is more abundant and work more regular, there is the angle of occupation of the country, now that aerial routes, mineral developments, and other reasons make possible the claims of other countries to part of Canada's Arctic, which now reaches to the North Pole.

To forestall any such future claims, the Dominion is occupying the Arctic islands to within nearly 700 miles of the North Pole. (J. Montagnes 1935: *Occupy Arctic Isles to Insure Canadian Claims*)

What was life like for those ten families and the families that subsequently followed them to the surrounding High Arctic locations? The government promised all of them that they could return home if the experiments failed, but many never saw home again. The 1934 Dundas Harbour experiment lasted two years before the government dismantled it. Marcus writes that the fifty-three men, women, and children were not sent home, but relocated to the north of Baffin Island to populate a proposed new trading post. He goes on to interview John Amagoalik who, at five, was part of the mid-1950s relocation experiment at Resolute. Amagoalik told him that Resolute, at the same latitude as Dundas Harbour, was so windswept and cold there wasn't enough snow to make snow houses, so the families wintered in tents. They were not used to months of darkness, and game was scarce: families were forced to raid the RCMP officers' garbage dump to scavenge half-eaten sandwiches. While at the dump, they were heartbroken to find a cache of letters—letters they had entrusted to the police to send to their loved ones back home—discarded among the garbage.

Bob Pilot was an RCMP officer in the High Arctic during those times. Marcus quotes him as having this to say about what he called the RCMP "flag detachments" in the Far North: "We were up there for one reason—sovereignty, and the Inuit were moved up there for the same reason."

* * *

THE DUNDAS HARBOUR RCMP station, scattered forlorn on the tundra, repelled me, and the reason for its being there in the first place — to maintain Arctic sovereignty for Canada — troubled me, as did our treatment of that as a thing noble and exalted. I hated prowling around the precincts, opening and closing old drawers, craning to read the note on how to fill the fuel drums, scrawled in the 1970s by crew members sent to check on the graves:

1. *Fill* 10 *Gal gas cans using hand pump.*
2. *Pour fuel out from* 10 *gal. cans into large bung hole of indoor fuel drum.*
3. 40 *gal. fuel oil lasts approx.* 5 *days' burning fuel on both heaters . . .*

The white pickets were fresh and upstanding: the RCMP and the Canadian Coast Guard weren't alone in maintaining them. As recently as 2006 they'd had help from sailors, infantry, Canadian Rangers, and the Prime Minister himself, who'd launched a twelve-day pageant to claim Arctic sovereignty that perhaps had less to do with dignity for the dead than with military exercises like those we had seen in Pond Inlet. Titled Operation Lancaster, the 2006 exercise had Aurora aircraft hover over Canadian military personnel who dismantled the Dundas Harbour cemetery fence and ceremonially placed newly painted pickets.

As I thought about how Canada had historically used Northern peoples and still used places like Dundas Harbour as symbolic markers of territory, I once again fell away from the others. A tiny red lichen spoke to me and I knelt and felt its warmth in the sun, listening to its quiet elocution of whispering green and plaited rust frond. I'd seen Aaju Peter fall away from the crowd like this and look at vegetation or listen to the silences that followed our procession. Earlier on the ship I'd heard her speak about territory and ownership in the North, and her point of view was not pinned to any kind of pomp or militaristic glory.

"Since we gave up our rights to this huge territory," she'd said, "the government has not fulfilled its obligations. They are not doing the work to fulfill their nice statements. Nunavut and all the northern territories should be provinces, with rights equal to provinces in the rest of Canada."

"What do you suggest?" asked Anna, an American.

"Education is the key. Inuit need to become active participants in decision-making, especially now, with the Northwest Passage opening and everyone—China, Russia—wanting to be players. Inuit can't just be onlookers."

"How will anything change?"

"We need a university in Nunavut. We are creating a university now, but it can't be the same as a southern university."

"That's true," said Bernadette, who'd been educated by white teachers who'd made her feel small, in a high school named after John Franklin. "Education has to incorporate our language. Our values."

As others scoured the RCMP site I left my piece of lichen and walked slowly, watching the ground which had begun to appear like a soft, breathing chest full of quiet secrets. Here

was another patch of lichen; here, a tiny, eight-petalled star-
flower on a cushion of red, green, and gold. Sheena had con-
vinced me to bring a small notebook out on the land, and a
pencil stub — not a proper drawing pencil, but an HB stub
tiny enough to fit in my pocket with the book. I began sketching — I could add colour later and had only to write initials
and abbreviated colour names: rust R., lime, chartreuse/gold,
midnight bl. w. green/gray. Here lay an interlocking line of
some mammoth beast's bleached spine, there a skull, here the
tiny, curved rib bone of a smaller animal hidden in yellow Arctic poppies.

I began to see that land in the Far North is undisturbed for
so many stretches of time that remnants we'd normally clear
away in the south become a visible testament, a word made out
of bone and metal or whatever material remains after the long
winters and summer winds. You can stand on the earth in the
Arctic and read stories through time, all visible together in the
great big, expansive now.

As I rounded an embankment, thinking these bones and
shards were about the past, I realized that atop the ridge huddled a herd of massive, woolly muskoxen, poised like one collective mountain of a body, full of warm and woebegone eyes,
regarding me motionless while their cascading wool moved
like shredded curtains against the sky.

So tiny were the Arctic lichen and grasses and buds that
fed the animals, yet so huge were the muskoxen, the whole
equation seemed impossible. These animals had nothing to do
with the human meaning for which we'd come to this spot.
No RCMP history or military exercise touched them. Or did it?

One of the jobs of the RCMP in the High Arctic was, according to Alan Marcus, to enforce game regulations that prohibited Inuit from hunting muskoxen. The measures were designed in the 1920s to stop Greenlandic Inuit from coming over to hunt in claimed Canadian territory; but for Inuit experiencing Canada's forced relocation experiments, the game laws compounded a life of hardship and starvation.

Now I confronted the living muskoxen around me. How ancient they appeared, and how my heart went out to them for their imperturbable stance up there on a ridge that belonged not to *us*, not to any government, but to them and their ancestors whose bones lay about the land aglow in a glory of light. How meek they were, how patient, waiting for miniature grasses and flowers to grow and become food.

Part of me was aware that the herd held back incredible strength: they were waiting, looking at us. In the absence of any stampede I heard their hooves thunder downhill — it felt part of human instinct to know what that would sound like, and how there'd be nothing one could do about it once the herd decided to run. I was in a crowd of British punks in 1980s Brixton, listening to a concert, when the crowd lunged and I went under, pinned in the mud as thousands of boots surged. A hand came from the sky and found mine and lifted me. It was the hand of a stranger who wore a purple Mohawk, leather, and chains. I asked him why he'd cared to reach down and save me.

"It's my last day as a punk."

"Why?"

"Got a job starting tomorrow. After this concert I'm going

for a haircut, and by this time tomorrow I'll be in an office in a shirt and tie." He was about to cry.

But he was not out here on the tundra. The muskoxen were not moving. I felt, instinctively: They are herbivores, and uninterested in eating meat off my bones. They charge to protect themselves or their young. They have been in this place thousands of years and are essentially wise and gentle.

The bodies, and the way they stood together, and what they said with their huge, knowing eyes, combined to tell me not to fear, to be respectful, and to move away without breaking their trust.

Instinct had visited me before, in a different wilderness. While berry picking on a high hill in Newfoundland when Esther was a newborn, I'd laid her in the bushes, thinking she could lie wrapped in her blanket as I filled my pail. But the instant I turned for the berries I felt a sudden sharp message that I knew instinctively as a threat from an eagle. I saw no eagle but knew it was there; it had seen my baby and could easily lift her to its hiding place in the cliffs, crash her down, pluck her eyes, and devour her flesh. Inaudible yet heard, this warning flashed through my body. Later, doubting that an eagle could steal a child, I went to the archives to look through old newspapers and see if I could find any instance of such a thing, and indeed — a family had lost its child to an eagle on that hill, in those bushes, nearly a hundred years before. To me time didn't matter in such stories.

Now, in Dundas Harbour with muskoxen who moved, living, among littered bones of their ancestors, I felt the land begin to speak louder than it spoke in cities. My own animal instinct came to the foreground of my being. It was not less complex or intelligent than ordinary thought with its linguistic structures, but it had a different kind of knowledge: deeper, older, more connected with my body, and in some palpable way connected also with the bodies of the tundra and the muskoxen themselves, with the ground a live conductor. The human settlement of the RCMP below the muskoxen's ridge was an unutterably lonely place and I could hardly bear it, but here with the animals and the tundra plants, I felt no loneliness.

THAT NIGHT, ON board our vessel, I saw that our ship's map now situated us north of Baffin Island, whose southern edge bore the Latin name *Meta Incognita*. The name was bestowed by Elizabeth I when Britain sent Martin Frobisher to find Arctic gold, long before Franklin. It implied a place beyond known limits, an unknown region to which humanity aspires in a philosophic sense. It thus evaded any connotation of a gold grab, hiding avarice behind a beautiful name that evoked how all of us wish we saw the world. *Meta Incognita* implied that state interest in Northern exploration was lofty: gain lay beyond any notion of money. As *Meta Incognita* persists on Canada's map, so the idea of a romantic, unattainable North remains in us even as governments accelerate efforts to establish sovereignty there.

I had witnessed Canada's military presence around Pond Inlet, Dundas Harbour, and other points on our route, and now began to see it as inseparable from historical campaigns whose quiet motivations lay veiled behind stories with more public appeal. Canada had recently begun to set much store on publicizing an invigorated and expensive search for the Franklin wrecks, while quietly using the same search technology to pursue soundings of the Arctic seafloor for data needed by oil consortiums, mineral concerns, and military interests. But the romance of the Franklin story was what made the news headlines. I began to question my own response to the North. Was the mysterious energy of the land real, or was my perception of it a romantic remnant from Franklin's day? What right had I to hold on to a romance—a lie of old kings and new leaders— to justify centuries of raid masquerading as an eternal hero's quest? My passage on the ship placed me inside this question. No matter how well-meaning the passengers, could we claim to stand apart from questions of invasion, privilege, and trespass?

Yet I felt a thrill—we all felt it—at being among the few southerners who'd ever set foot in what we call the Far North. The notion of beyond, our *Meta Incognita*, was still part of our consciousness. We were not Bernadette Dean or Aaju Peter, who lived in the North and whose people had done so longer than any British explorer with insufficient pantaloons, lost ships, or lonesome graves. How strange to experience being "beyond known limits" while realizing this very notion was a dream. Even the word "North" began to dissolve: once you were here, that territory became something else: unnamed, and real unto itself.

We were a moving, borderless collection of our own dreams and imagination, and the place acted on us with shifting meanings that altered with the hours. There was a mutability about our time in the tundra, rock, ice: solid forms that colluded with each other to act more like thought and water.

chapter twelve

THE WHITE GARDEN

As we left Dundas Harbour and headed for the place British explorers had called Beechey Island, I felt part of a mythology about which I was becoming more and more uneasy. The Northwest Passage is itself a colonial code name: Bernadette Dean had implied the term was faintly ridiculous in her view, and also dismissive and threatening. No one, she said, who lives in the North calls the place by that name—only those who view the land as something they can turn into money.

I'd tacitly agreed to that colonial view when I embarked on our voyage. The names we give things betray who we are. This territory was "northwest" in relation to what? What made it a passage? England, Queen Victoria, the Johns Franklin and Rae, and all the other Johns? Knickerbockers and breeches, hounds and pianofortes? Certainly it remains northwest in relation to southeast England, where Vita Sackville-West's famous white garden glows at night, butter-white, filled with poetry, English class structure, and cultivars of rose and lime. And "passage" — why must we pass through land, dismissing and conquering it? What if we were to stay in one place, get to know it, and listen? What might happen if we were not always on our way somewhere else?

On our voyage I'd begun to see from a point of view other than the one I'd inherited from my ancestors and Eurocentric education. Bernadette Dean and Aaju Peter had seen to that, and the terrain also spoke from its own point of view. I no longer wanted to call it the Northwest Passage, but Tundra, Place of Northern Lights, Nunavut's Coast, or some other name of its own. Or, better yet, let it remain unnamed. The idea of a northwest passage insinuated a connection between earth's corporeality and mine in a way I found discomfiting. "She" was a place inviolate and mysterious, protected by ice, darkness, and strange patterns of day so indecipherable to Franklin and his men they died trying to charge through her. Subjugation and shame wash over conquered ground: land, people, animals, and plants may ask, "Who tramples? Who trespasses?" but are made to feel they're imagining things.

What did John Franklin carry on board his lost ship? He took chocolate, candles, and the best furnishings his age had to offer. He took scientific apparatus for botanical and geological experiments. A library of a thousand books and a barrel organ. He clung to the trappings of his own culture.

When my mother and I visited England a few years ago, she wanted to see her northern seaside hometown and I wanted to see Vita Sackville-West's white garden at Sissinghurst Castle. In my mother's South Shields we stayed in a bed and breakfast where the employees slapped beans, sausage, and eggs on plates in the morning. They crashed around the kitchenette as we drank our coffee, and they couldn't wait to get off their shifts. My mother seemed comfortable with this, and with the local fish and chip shops, curry takeouts, and the fairground. But when we reached our next accommodations, one of seven guestrooms in the old gardener's house at Sissinghurst, she became uneasy.

I liked the old couple who ran the place. They owned a black lab and the house bore a perpetual scent of damp dog. It rained and the couple was grateful when I offered to walk the dog around the gardens under their giant black umbrella. Our room was a hymn to shabby grandeur, with an old claw-foot tub and handmade lace antimacassars, and the breakfast was glorious: homemade marmalade, toast in a silver rack with a warming cloth; herring, boiled eggs, cheeses, and fruit; scones and fresh butter; coffee and pots of red-hot tea. None of it felt pretentious to me; it felt sedate, quiet, and spacious, with a faded elegance. I felt I could have moved in and lingered there forever, writing and reading and pausing for cups of tea; but I saw my mother fidget, judging, longing to get out, and I guessed her discomfort came from an inner tension that had to do with something rattling and gnawing in her Old World blood.

I was full of contradiction: I felt comfortable in the castle gardens, dining on blackberry preserves — the toast thin, the preserves tart so as to release the purity of fruit on the bush in an English summer. I loved the dog, wet and smelly, for he was a hunting dog who tenderly clamped his jaw around the master's shot duck, never breaking the flesh with his trembling fangs, impeccably trained. I loved the large, black umbrella with the civilized drizzle falling on it, so unlike the driving sleet of Newfoundland. In England, especially in the south, I felt protected and at home. Yet the lure of a wilderness that had called my father also called me. I cared little about the histories of the particular Irish, English, or Scottish settlers who came before my family to the New World. What I cared about were the things for which they came: mystic wilderness, magnetic north, charged space filled with possibility and illumined by the aurora borealis.

Outside the castle and the gardener's house stood the walled gardens of Vita and her husband Harold Nicolson, whose unorthodox marriage was mirrored in the intricate contortions of lime trees, roses, and hedges — but I wanted to see the famous white garden, for which Vita had cultivated shades of snow and cream, pale greens and greys. It never failed that each summer, at the height of colour and fertility, I felt a torpor, and I loved the idea of settling summer's fervour with cooling white.

After our magnificent breakfast my mother and I walked to a freestanding booth that reminded me of an antique and glorified telephone kiosk, the way Dr. Who's TARDIS might have appeared in 1851 had it touched down at England's Great Exhibition in the Crystal Palace. Inside sat a perfect little man in a uniform with shining buttons, from whom we were to buy tickets to see the garden. He was so proper, so in and of his station, that I felt astonished when, as I turned away, he called after me.

"Excuse me, Ma'am?"

I knew that, in England, this was what you called the Queen, instead of the more familiar "Madam." Every banister I'd ever slid down faded away. This man was a real English-man and knew how to address women who'd eaten kippers and were about to step into white gardens. He was unlike men of the New World. Our Newfoundland premier, as evidenced during a recent visit by Her Majesty, could have used a lesson from him. The premier had committed the unpardonable sin of attempting to help the Queen up a set of St. John's stairs by planting his hand on her coat to steady the royal bottom. I'd gasped. It had been on the news. Normally, when men in or out of booths address me, I ignore them, as my mother taught. One day she was walking down Valley Road in Corner Brook and one of my brothers saw her from a way off. She ignored him and he whistled. She delivered him a lecture on how no woman under any circumstances should have to suffer being called in that manner. She failed to see how she'd managed to raise a son who didn't know this in every capillary of his being without being told.

"Ma'am?"

Did I dare turn and see what the man in the TARDIS wanted? My mother wasn't far. She might come running to hit him over the head.

"Yes?"

He leaned meekly: angels might smite him. He glanced at heavens north and south, blushing.

"Ma'am, I only wanted...If you wouldn't mind my say-ing, but when you took your ticket, I noticed . . ."

I looked down; maybe I'd dropped a pound note.

"You have such a beautiful smile. I'm ever so sorry, I hope you don't mind." He ducked like a frightened mouse.

The mouse's compliment accompanied me to the white garden, where I stood under brick arches studying *Dianthus* and *Stachys lanata*, cream peonies and white irises, *Onopordum* and *Malva*. Vita Sackville-West's garden was about quietness — a thing I loved and did not want violated.

Now, on our journey through the North with its own vast quietness, I had no wish to charge through: men had already done this. My goal was not to colonize or subjugate the body of land. Or was it?

There existed at least two lands in the one body through which we sailed: the land lusted-for and ludicrously named by European ancestors, and another unknown to colonists — a body that had swallowed Franklin and now nurtured muskoxen, lichen, and the humans it chose to love. We were about to intrude on Beechey Island using cultural implements similar to the ones Franklin carried on his lost ship and cultural attitudes very like the ones he'd carried in his mind. I carried the colonial folly English people inherit whether they like it or not, and did not see how I would escape it.

My mother told me her own mother, the daughter of a ship owner, was disinherited following her marriage to my grandfather, a man ten years younger than herself without education, money, or a trade. I remember going into a shop where he worked: metal house-numbers hung on a carousel and there was a key-cutting machine. I know he had periods of no work. When my mother was a child her mother often gave her a note and said run across town to Auntie Hilda's house, and Hilda would read the note then wrap half a crown in it and send it back. An incendiary bomb blackened the dining table during the war, and after the war it was never repaired, right up until the time my mother married and left home. But that table was always set with flatware and a silver teapot stand I now possess, and the table setting was more like the one in the gardener's house at Vita's castle than in the working-class kitchen at our South Shields inn.

My mother's father wore a bowler hat and spoke of himself in the third person: "Your grandad has not been given one of the nice new flats overlooking the Roman ruins, but has been put on a waiting list for some ordinary flats, of all things — can you imagine? Your grandad on a waiting list?"

Even as a child I knew lots of people went on waiting lists and wondered why my grandad should be any different, but he didn't see it that way. My mother told me that when he came back from the war he gave her a ring he said he'd found on the grounds of Buckingham Palace.

"I never questioned it," she said. "I was a child. Buckingham Palace! I believed him. Then one day when I was old, I mean I must have been in my twenties, or at least eighteen or nineteen, I casually told one of my friends that my dad had, you know, that he'd found this ring on the palace grounds, and, well, I must have been so naïve, but that's the way I was. And when my friend said it wasn't possible, but ludicrous, no one finds a ring on the grounds of Buckingham Palace, I . . ." My mother trailed off and I saw how sad this story made her feel even now, her dad long gone and herself married in Canada with grown children and grandchildren.

This tension followed me to Newfoundland, where there were no palaces with or without rings strewn on their grounds. My mother asks me periodically if I still possess her mother's silver teapot stand, as if she fears some barbaric gene might cause me to chuck it. One of my mother's favourite activities, and mine, is to pick around second-hand shops hunting sterling among the costume jewelry, spying English hand-painted dishes with 22-karat gold edges, nabbing Italian merino garments and shirts of the finest silk like those in old songs. We bring these things home for pennies and use them as if no one had disowned anybody in my mother's past; as if neither of us ever had to think about money.

"Money," my mother told me, in one of her pronouncements out of the earshot of anyone else, "is power."

"Some of your mother's people," my father said, "were snobs." His own father had been a limelight lad in theatre productions, a boxer whose face got bashed in so many times he told everyone he stopped the buses with his nose. My father's mother told fortunes with tea leaves and cards and made money telling her neighbours who would meet a dark stranger, who might soon conceive twins, and who'd get five pieces of money in a letter from far away.

I loved my fortune-telling grandmother in a way that my mother could not. "We do not," my mother informed her, "shout from one room in the house to a person in another room. We do not shout out the windows to a family member in the street. We do not let the dog in the house when it is raining and there's mud on his paws." There were other commandments: we did not discuss our aches and pains, bunions on our feet, or darker bodily functions. Nor did we have superstitions of any kind, or believe the Jack of Spades or any other card meant a dark stranger, a visit from the postman, or a knock on our door by Death. We did not wear great big rhinestone brooches in our hats, and we certainly didn't own wigs or false teeth, and we did not go to Woolworths every Saturday to replenish our supply of lemon bonbons for our diabetes. We did not have chronic bronchitis and did not melt candles in the shapes of our enemies or give them names and keep them in the pantry with pins stuck in them. At least my mother did not, and she tried energetically to bequeath these standards to me. But I became someone who hoards a stash of rhinestones that would make my grandma proud. I keep Tarot cards in my writing room, and if I don't make wax effigies or hurl curses on my enemies it's because I choose not to unleash the Furies.

One of the letters my grandmother sent me on airmail parchment said: "I will soon be getting my old age pension. When I get it, I will be able to go on the buses free. I'm going to go everywhere on those buses. Morpeth, Shields, Gateshead. I'm going to ride like a queen. I must go now because they have pork roasts on sale at the butcher. Pork roast costs an arm and a leg. But you only live once. Love, Grandma."

I became interested in class and socio-economic territory, intrigued by doors that allowed or barred entry to certain worlds — especially since the doors became invisible or reappeared depending on who sought or didn't seek them. I suspected that being an artist might be a way to materialize the doors. I know one who lives on apples and day-old bread but who, because of her spellbinding work, gets invited to the

Lieutenant Governor's annual garden party. She drapes a rose tablecloth across her shoulder, cinches it with a diamond clasp from an old lover's great aunt, then knocks back bellyfuls of His Honour's caviar.

Approaching Beechey Island, I watched for doors visible and invisible. I spied doors below deck where our Philippine crew shared bare-bones cabins. Daily at four, Mariana — she'd written her name on a card — turned my sheets and placed that chocolate on my pillow. At dinner, if the swell sent salt pots sliding over the tables, our waiters lifted fruit and coffee urns high, their bodies transformed into *balançoires*. There was a head chef, a bread chef, a dessert chef, a fish chef, a breakfast chef, and a pastry chef, and after one particular dinner they and their assistants all appeared carrying, on their heads, ice cream mousses carved into icebergs: they wove among our tables, portioning the ice cream and finally standing shyly as we applauded. Certain passengers read the crew's nametags and addressed them familiarly, though the passengers themselves wore no tags, and others appeared to ignore the servers: their food lowered itself to their place settings by undetectable means. What was I to make of my own presence on this ship, I wondered, as I remembered my two grandmothers, one of whom would have known how to collect her turtle broth by tipping a soup spoon backwards, and the other who might have scrubbed the floors, wheezing and rubbing ointment on her bunions while the paying guests slumbered?

chapter thirteen

BEECHEY ISLAND

BEECHEY ISLAND IS the bleakest, most desolate piece of land I have ever seen. Covered in limestone rubble, its flat shore stretches a monochromatic grey that hardly rises from the water until rock heaves up suddenly behind the beach. The grave markers of Franklin's crewmen John Torrington, John Hartnell, and William Braine jut from the stones. The three were the first men to die on Franklin's lost expedition, and their tilting gravestones are one of European Arctic history's most iconic and haunting legacies. This site is a place of closing chapters, a shutting down of Franklin's hopes and the hopes of England. No shrub, no flower: even lichen has diminished to a whisper on this beach that isn't a beach in any English sense at all, but a wasteland. Time has embalmed an atmosphere of doom.

Our anoraks blared red, yellow, and blue. The colours rang hollow as we stepped around the graves, feeling the ground might drain us into itself.

"Please," I heard Nathan ask a passenger, "don't walk right there. Those stones—we all need to remember these are real graves, and I ask you respectfully … we need to desist from walking on them, it's very important. These are sacred remains."

I wanted to get away from the graves, and started toward the water's edge where at least there was movement and sound, even if only a frill of water on stones.

Someone from the gun perimeter shouted: urgent crackling from the walkie-talkie of one of our expedition leaders. What was he shouting? The stones and vast space swallowed detail; people murmured until word reached me just as I saw— at the end of Beechey Island—a polar bear.

"Get back to the Zodiacs," an assistant pleaded. "Please do not think you can hang around and watch the bear. Please immediately return to the beach and the Zodiacs will take you back to the ship."

He sounded calm, but I knew he spoke from that place where all you can think about is how close you might be to death, either your own or that of those for whom you are responsible. We were a crowd whose age averaged close to seventy: many were world travellers but had come with telescopic canes or dietary restrictions. One was blind, and Motoko remained on crutches after her fall in Greenland. We were a crowd of pilgrims who had, collectively, paid more than a million dollars to come close to a polar bear.

The bear was a cream-coloured patch one minute, but the next he was close enough that our biologist could tell us, "He's a male … and he's hungry."

Zodiacs bobbed at the shoreline and people began board-ing them — our ship waited far enough off that I found myself counting how many trips the Zodiacs needed to make, and whether we had enough time.

I fell between those who wanted to escape the island and those hanging back to risk seeing the bear more closely. As he grew near I saw Aaju Peter kneel on the stones with her rifle, looking the bear directly in the eye. Passengers down on the shore crowded hurriedly for the second round of Zodiacs. I knew I shouldn't linger but was fascinated by how Aaju knelt, her strength and intensity and no-nonsense directness. What was she saying to the bear?

In a third round of Zodiacs photographers floated as close to shore as they could, lenses massive against the stones, lichen, and breaths of cloud. How loudly blared those colours of our anoraks. They were part of the paraphernalia I tried to ignore. But without all our props — without the dinghies and the gear and our expedition leaders — we wouldn't have been here in the first place, and even if we had somehow arrived without them we'd have fallen or been swallowed or frozen or submerged long before we saw this polar bear. We'd have starved, or had the flesh peeled from our bones by forces that had left bones all over this terrain.

I realized Aaju was singing. The point of our gun perim-eter was to enable our party to shoot a predator if we had to, and we were closer to doing so than any of us had anticipated. I listened as Aaju sang to the bear, which had, in very few minutes, covered nearly two kilometres and was now less than one kilometre from us. Aaju sang an Inuit song, and my body heard and understood what she would confirm when I asked her about it later.

"I sang," she told me, "to let the bear know he should not be afraid. I promised him that we meant to leave him alone on his island, with the graves."

While she sang, I prayed we would not have to shoot the bear. What right did we have to kill an animal who had been minding his own business, here on his lonely island away from all white people except for Franklin's dead men and our invading selves? The last thing any of us wanted was to end the bear's magnificent life.

Aaju steadfastly sang to the bear and as she sang to him I watched. His magnificence filled me with a kind of desperation. If we were forced to kill the bear it would mean we had exchanged his life for ours, when he had done nothing to invite us here or to threaten anybody. We were the ones who had encroached on his terrain. And what right did we have to do even that? I felt the weight and enormity of his life, the power of his aliveness welling out and intersecting with my own. His dignity filled me with an emotion I had not experienced and could not name.

THAT NIGHT IN the lounge Nathan performed. Everyone was still excited about the bear, and between songs they talked of nothing else.

"He was a bit thin."

"No, he was fairly well-fed."

"Does anyone know how old he was?"

"Pierre said he was three years old, maybe four."

"How many metres away from us would you say he came?"

"I heard the expedition leader say that was the closest he or anyone on the staff has ever come to a polar bear on land. My husband says if it had taken us three more minutes to leave the island . . ."

Near the end of his set Nathan spied me backing away from the crowd, getting ready to escape to my cabin, and after the song he came over.

"Hey. You okay?"

I barely held back tears.

"The bear?"

I nodded.

"He affected you big-time."

"I can't stop thinking about him."

"I can see that."

"Not the facts about his weight or his age, or measuring how close he came. I'm thinking about his life on that island, when none of us is around."

"I know."

chapter fourteen

FOLLOWING FRANKLIN

I CONSULTED THE daily expedition sheet that had been slipped, as always, under our cabin doors before wake-up call. It was Day Nine, a Sunday, and we were scheduled to travel down Prince Regent Inlet to Bellot Strait, the first place Pacific and Atlantic waters meet anywhere north of Tierra del Fuego. Much of what Europeans had longed for in a Northwest Passage is symbolized here: on the map it's a thread, undetected for centuries of Arctic exploration and unknown in Europe until Saskatchewan-born fur trader William Kennedy, whose mother was Cree, found it while leading Jane Franklin's 1851 search for her husband's remains.

I lay on my bunk and thought about the bear and about the land we had seen so far. I knew the Beechey Island graves of Torrington, Hartnell, and Braine had lain in the perma-frost since 1846 when Franklin buried them. I'd seen images of the men's agonized grimaces; when I thought of them now I felt horrified. Before Canadian forensic anthropologist Owen Beattie exhumed the men in 1984, no one had seen their mummified faces. They remained an idea, abstract and ghostly. But now I had seen both the images and the graves: I would be a corpse one day and I hoped I'd never reach that state of exposure and desolation.

I relived the tundra we had walked—the muskoxen, the bear, and the tiny, miraculous Arctic plants. I saw the sky, vast and mackerel-clouded one day, flawless the next, pulsing at night with that blue Arctic glow. Something had happened to me—it had begun in Dundas Harbour and intensified on Beechey Island: a new exchange between the ground and my body. The animals, the land, and the air around them had begun to transmit something new to me. Even in the northernmost south, we tend to ascribe meaning chiefly to things that have been removed from their elemental state. We layer sign on sign: map-making, street signs, architecture, and embellishment. Signs communal and individual amass into strata of meaning more dense and significant to us than the unsignposted terrain of wild places, or of our inner selves. Now, though, I began to feel the Arctic as palpably different in essence and identity from how I normally interpreted land.

I'd been conditioned in the south to locate thought inside myself, the same model of perception that fuelled early European exploration, science and reason: thinking conducted inside a skull looking out at an external world. But was this true? I'd come to the Arctic at a moment's notice with nothing but the required items on the baggage list and my inherited way of seeing. But the ice, the bear, the muskoxen, and the whole elemental place had changed this perception. They spoke without audible sound but with a powerful urgency that made me question the nature of what I had known as thought.

Was the land suggesting that here, in the Arctic, we do not own or contain individual thought, but rather move in a living element that contains us? Was it possible this living element was, itself, conscious? Were the sky over the tundra, and the lakes where muskoxen drank, a mind-substance into which I'd moved, as an imagined form might enter someone's thoughts? Were my body and the terrain — the green and yellow tundra, the purple and white mountains, the lichen and stones — parts of one and the same body?

I knew I'd come deep into a presence of an Arctic majesty that possessed no trappings, no charts, no commandments in stone. It spoke no audible word, yet I heard its message and felt a current. A communication from the earth had begun to infiltrate me in a way that was different from how I normally intercepted things. Here, in the waters under my rocking bed and in the land around us, hummed a sentience larger than mine. Between my body and the bodies of land and water hummed communication — a message in the combined body that broke my solitude and connected me with the North's living energy.

The day's expedition sheet also said we'd be visiting the Hudson Bay Company's last trading post, named after John Ross. Ross had explored Lancaster Sound in 1818, looking for the Northwest Passage, but he turned home after encountering an impenetrable mountain range that proved to be a mirage. Fort Ross was built in 1937 to bridge the eastern and western Arctic fur trading districts and abandoned ten years later when company employees and Inuit families were moved south to Spence Bay, or Taloyoak.

But as the morning progressed, our plans changed for the same reason that Fort Ross was abandoned all those years ago: Bellot Strait was unnavigable. Then and now, ice blocked the strait. So instead of turning south down Prince Regent Inlet, our captain decided we would sail around Somerset Island's north shore and then travel down its western coast along Peel Sound. This meant our journey would be taking a shape neither Ken McGoogan nor our expedition leaders had experienced before. We were embarking on the exact route Franklin had taken toward King William Island, where his ships, *Erebus* and *Terror*, became fatally icebound.

We all loved the idea that things were not going as planned. We had the perfect situation required by the human soul according to Maslow's hierarchy of needs — that pyramid with food and safety at its base, a sense of belonging in the centre, and, at the top, a pinnacle with labels that included creative problem solving, spontaneity, and an unprejudiced embracing of new information. The fragility of our physical comfort made comfort's continued existence all the more exquisite. Yes, we knew we were in a little boat whose frame was like a seashell floating in the vastness. We knew it could succumb at any time to the same unforeseen perils that had plagued or killed real Arctic explorers, perils Bernadette Dean continually reminded me existed now: ice, storms, rogue tides, and ravenous omnivores. But I nudged those dangers toward the edges of our voyage like winds and ghosts in my childhood nursery rhyme book that portrayed Wynken, Blynken, and Nod sailing off in their wooden shoe. Those pages, illustrated with silvery herring, silken nets, and an old moon who asked the three voyagers their wishes, blazed gold and amethyst at their centre. Shadows remained at a safe distance and could not touch the dreaming sailors. It was easy for me to imagine how John Ross might have spied a whole gleaming mountain range that didn't exist, and how he could have believed in it — though some of his men asked him to investigate further before succumbing to the illusion — enough to give it a name, Croker's Mountains, after the British Secretary to the Admiralty. While Ross was at it he named the cape to the south of the mirage after British Foreign Secretary Viscount Castlereagh, a name that might conjure Fata Morganas and other castles in the air — were it not for the fact that Castlereagh ended up going mad, slitting his throat, and having both Shelley and Lord Byron write vitriolic verses about him.

We were in a place where mountains might or might not exist, names of capes and inlets changed according to who observed them, and ice formed, melted, or moved: so it was no surprise that our own voyage should have plans that metamorphosed. There was a flicker of excitement as the crew advised us to discard the itinerary paper. The sheet became evidence of a route not taken, though it had been envisioned as carefully as the imaginary mountains of John Ross.

The frisson in the dining room swept over the table where I sat eating breakfast with Nathan. "I feel a new thing happening," he said, "now that we've gone off the planned route. I feel we're going to find something."

I caught the excitement. Maybe we'd be the first people in

Arctic exploration to see Franklin's bones shining underwater. I pictured them green-glimmering-white, floating from where they'd lain, unmoored at last by some accident of tide or ice. Across the dining room Bernadette Dean talked with a Philippine crew member and I thought of what she would say: that all thought of finding Franklin was a ridiculous relic from dead glories of the British empire. What's more, I'd agree with her. And yet, and how strange: I felt a vestigial thrill.

I thought of the Montreal neighbourhood to which we had moved from Newfoundland: brick houses built in the mid-1900s by Italian, Greek, and Portuguese immigrants. The residents are old now, but they still rent out upstairs rooms and keep house on the ground floors and plant European vegetable gardens in the back alleys, or *ruelles*: eggplant, tomatoes, opulent gourds suspended from lattices improvised out of broom handles and the old hockey sticks their children learned to use in the new winter country. When he rented our house to us, our Italian landlord, who lives in the suburbs, told us that his parents, beloved on the street, had kept two fig trees and Concord grapevines in the backyard. He wanted to transplant the vines, get rid of the fig trees, and put in a parking space.

"The figs are great," he said, "slit open, stuffed with blue cheese, and flung on the barbecue. But they're a ton of work."

Each autumn, he told us, the trees had to be dug around the root ball, then toppled and laid in the hole of a giant trench — which also required digging — and buried under a few feet of soil. In spring there was a resurrection — you dug the trees up again and settled them upright with fertilizer, just as Christ advised in the Gospels of Matthew and Mark.

"Nobody," said our landlord, "wants to do that kind of work anymore."

"We do," we said, and he left the trees for us to tend. We soon learned that our Greek neighbour across the alley—a man named Theophanos, whose luxuriant moustache shot out several inches then curled skyward—also had a fig tree, and he and our landlord's late father had practiced a biennial ritual of burying and resurrecting the trees. We began to do this together, and my husband took to visiting Theo and eating orange segments in homemade syrup, and sweet Cypriot cakes with strong coffee, and fresh curd cheese with oregano. He learned a few Greek words, most of which meant "Take it easy" or "go slowly." I liked hearing about all of it, but my favourite linguistic discovery came when my husband returned from an espresso break to tell me what Theo called English people. There were Greek nicknames, it appeared, for all the minorities in our immigrant quarter, but the English had a special one.

"Guess what it is."

My husband and I like making each other guess things. We get three guesses, then a clue, and one last chance. I have a pretty respectable record—and in Montreal, there were already a lot of things I'd heard Anglos called.

"Clock-watchers?"

"Nope."

"Um…horsefaces?"

"You're not really in the right ballpark."

"Teapot-heads?"

"You're a bit closer."

"It has something to do with tea?"

"It has something to do with a sweet thing that English people consume."

"Battenberg cake? Sugar mice?"

"What the hell are sugar mice?"

"Marzipan?"

"Right initial, wrong word. You've had your three guesses."

"Mince tarts?"

"*Marmalados.*" My husband giggled. As a francophone Quebecois he finds marmalade ridiculous, especially since he knows I'll travel across town to the Atwater Market to get it, and he likes to scoff when I complain there's never lemon marmalade, only ginger or orange.

"*Marmalados!*"

I had to admit, it was perfect. It was a nickname I could enjoy being called. It had a pirate ring and was not far-fetched or untrue. If I was anything I was a *Marmalado*. I tried it out on my friend Ross. He too was delighted. We were *Marmalados* in a world of francophones and Greeks with their Brie and eggplant, their *sirop d'érable* and their nightshades whose tendrils crept through the alleys at night. Other ethnicities had their fascinating trappings and now so did we *Marmalados* . . .

But what did it mean? No orange tree grows in England. *Marmalados*, I realized, perfectly illustrated England's history of colonial empire: ships bound for Seville and endless tallyhoing forth from William Blake's "dark Satanic mills" to some land, some place, where such a thing as oranges hung on trees, golden and aflame with exotic oil, bursting with juice and life unattainable in England's grey backyard. *Marmalados* pointed at British wanderlust: braving peril and discomfort in the name of finding that which fills body and soul with excitement. *Marmalados* are people who can't stop stealing other people's oranges and bringing them home in ships, crystallizing exotic experience to taste on spoons near coal fires along the Tyne or the Thames and other sullen rivers meandering leaden past English cobblestones and chimney pots. *Marmalados* go looking for the colour orange in a world of drizzle. They can't help it. They know real life is out there, somewhere beyond England, and their whole economy is about bringing home the ecstatic fruits.

On our own ship of imagining, Ken McGoogan leaned over his notes, his enthusiasm for our newly altered journey acquiring extra voltage. He had a way of wheeling his arms and flinging a hand toward this or that portentous height of land as he explained who'd overwintered or been the first colonial explorer to set foot there.

". . . years this August . . ." I heard him tell one of the geologists, ". . . wintered on Beechey . . . made a run down Peel Sound . . . The ships were waiting for Franklin, but he never arrived."

The North engenders lots of stories about white men who perish there, fables told and retold by those at home on safer shores. There they go in their bloomers, never bothering to ask any of the Inuit who come near their scurvy-ridden misery how a person might live through another frozen twenty-four hours. In Labrador there's a story of how Leonidas Hubbard and his 1903 expedition for an American magazine took the wrong turn, leading to his death as his small party subsisted on caches of mouldy peameal until they stumbled home. Like the Franklin stories, the Hubbard details have been rewritten in book after book, including one by Hubbard's wife, Mina, who retraced the route in a race with Hubbard's surviving expedition-mate Dillon Wallace, who'd written his own book, one Mina did not like. To this day urban canoeists and journalists persist in attempts to replicate the Hubbard expedition: many of them write their own books or articles, and somehow every word of this commands fascination even though the entire route has, since long before Hubbard's day, been amply sown with traces of Inuit camps and evidence that any Labrador-born hunter or trapper would have no trouble getting from Hamilton Inlet to Ungava Bay. What is so compelling about these expeditions?

Mina Hubbard retraced the route with George Elson, a Cree-Scot who'd been the guide of her husband and Dillon Wallace on the fatal journey. There remains enough implied sexual tension in accounts of their journey together to capture plenty of interest. We love to imagine what might happen between a man and a woman alone in the wilderness, especially when race, class, era, and gender forbid them to even converse in public. Then there was George Elson's prophetic dream, recounted in Wallace's book, in which prior to Hubbard's death George dreamed he saw Jesus, shining and bright, telling the men to stay on Beaver River where they'd find a certain "Blake" who had "plenty of grub — You'll be all right then boys, you'll be home safe." It turned out a man named Blake did have a cabin farther down Beaver River, but Hubbard did not listen to his Cree guide's dream.

So the Hubbard tale became imbued with forbidden romance and forsaken spiritual guidance from a colloquial Christ. A similar atmosphere pervaded Franklin's story, except Franklin's reached wider than Hubbard's. Instead of a journalist's sponsored trip that went wrong, the Franklin story involved, and continues to involve, queens, navies, and the sovereignty of nations each laying claim to a place beyond any world they've known. The Franklin story embodies romance while allowing past and contemporary powers to lay claim to the land that took his bones.

The American magazine that sponsored Hubbard's deadly expedition was called *Outing*. It began as a cycling magazine and evolved into a monthly study of everything to do with independent adventure travel, including to remote northern regions. While Mina Hubbard worked on her account of retracing her husband's journey, the magazine serialized Jack London's *White Fang*. From Yukon stories to Mina's *A Woman's Way Through Unknown Labrador*, the North continued to mean the greatest "outing" of all, the most "unknown" terrain, and it still does—although, as I was finding out, there are layers of truth and untruth to this, concealed in layers of geology, archaeology, and historical record.

What did it mean that we were, for the first time in the history of our own ship's officers and crew, travelling the exact route of the lost Franklin voyage? The more I thought about it, the more excited I felt. This wasn't just a chance to see Franklin's bones or other relics of his voyage. It was our own passage through a cache where the collective unconscious of *Marmalados* lies dreaming, remembering, and being re-dreamed. The more we walked the land, the more I realized that the ground and its people, animals, and plants had something they wanted us to add to the ideas we held and shared about the North.

We disembarked halfway down Peel Sound at a place called False Strait. There was mist, and the birders among us were excited about searching for the red-throated loon. I walked on a rocky shore in fog, enjoying the damp air on my face and a rare softness of light after so many days of bright Arctic sunshine. I left the main group of birders, unaware I was approaching a quiet passenger who may have known more about birds than any of the others with their gigantic cameras, tripods, and super-modern scopes. I saw her just as I was about to turn back to the ship. We now shadowed Franklin's route exactly and I did not want my bones to mingle with the bones of his men.

The quiet passenger was one of the Japanese charges of Yoko, my cabin mate. She'd walked the rocky contours, but now we were late in the afternoon and she was tiring — Yoko had told me some of her passengers were "very old" — and I asked if she'd like to walk with me. She held my arm and we navigated the rocks, which became elevated and difficult to see as the mist thickened. She told me she was looking, like others, for the red-throated loon. But unlike the birders who clicked shutters and ticked species off checklists, she appeared to want the loons' company. She and the loons were old acquaintances with news to catch up on. Her name was Junko, like the name of a bird I'd known in Newfoundland: a little grey junco who built her nest under grass, hidden in a strip of wild meadow between balsam fir trees and the sea.

We came around the last bluff to find the others on the main beach enacting a ceremony around a fifty-year-old cairn. The cairn had been built during a survey expedition by members of the U.S. Coastguard and the Canadian Hydrographic Service; a jar inside it contained a list of those visitors, and we were adding a record of our visit before replacing the jar. Ken McGoogan's enthusiasm for the cairn had people in thrall. Junko and I heard the group begin singing "The Northwest Passage"; I looked for Nathan but couldn't see him. Above us loomed rocks, and over the rocks gathered low mist and an empty sky. The song was mournful for a lot of reasons, and I wondered if Nathan might have fled. It didn't surprise me that he, who had begun fasting, listening, waiting for the place to speak to him, had removed himself at that moment. I didn't know what he felt, or if he heard the passengers singing his father's song from a distance, or if he didn't hear it at all, or was absent by happenstance, caught in a pocket of rock elsewhere on the shore. I do know I looked for Nathan at that moment and felt glad he wasn't there.

Our ship glimmered in the mist. Junko thanked me for helping her over the rocks.

"I wrote a book in Japan," she said, "about loons. I have some of my writing on the ship. I will give you a copy."

In fact Junko Momose had written extensively on wild birds; she was an expert in northern cultural and naturalist knowledge in Japan, and on the board of directors of a society dedicated to such knowledge. She had, in short, spent a lifetime acquainting herself with birds, notably loons, and especially the red-throated loon the birders on our ship longed to see. When I retired to my cabin that night Yoko handed me a slim blue book Junko had asked her to give me. It was a scientific paper, yet also a document of dreams, old stories, and imagination the likes of which I'd never seen. I marvelled as I lay reading it and looking at its maps and drawings: who could have known such a world of loon magic existed?

The book was about loon fishing, and as it revealed itself to me I thought it even more entrancing than Picasso's *Night Fishing at Antibes*, a painting I went back to again and again in my youth for its mystery, its fishermen with their lanterns, its jewel-like fish, and an ocean full of mysterious activity — purples and blues that signalled a dream universe. So much about that painting is indirect: I loved the fish lured by lanterns instead of bait alone. A woman on a bicycle watches. Is she eating an ice cream? The fish are snipped from disparate visions and one fisherman dangles his line from one foot. The colours, a vivid spiralling moon, and the conversation of paint, water, music, and people, suggest deep story, a dialogue through time. Junko's book on Japanese loon fishing had a similar effect on me. It incorporated drawing, observations excerpted from her diary, and a story about loons and fishers cooperating in an old choreography that was utilitarian yet filled with grace and magic.

There was a place in Japan called the Inland Sea where loons wintered. They were afraid of men, yet knew how to make the first link in a glittering chain that could make a fisherman rich.

I'd seen inshore fishers off the southeast coast of Newfoundland mend nets by hand in their kitchens and set off at dawn past the bird islands to their cod grounds. I knew there were shoals and dangers, skills they'd learned from grandfathers; secrets trawler fishers and big boatmen couldn't know. Before ultrasound, the old men knew where cod lay hiding. They teased the cod until the cod leapt on the jigger. But I'd never heard of anything like Japanese loon fishers.

As we sailed down Franklin Strait I lay on my bunk and read of the little wooden rowboats in which they went to see the loons. The men began in December, gently and slowly, without fishing a single fish, merely easing closer to the loons, floating quietly so the loons might admit the men into their company. For a month they floated, never once catching a fish, only waiting.

The loons circled shoals of little fish called sand lances that spawned in the sand like the glittering caplin I'd known. Loons circled the lances and fishermen circled the loons, never taking a fish. They rowed clockwise, congruent with currents and tides, like a round dance or circling moons. The loons corralled each shoal of lances, making it concentrate until dense enough so the loons could dive into the shoal and devour their fill. The fishermen waited.

They waited until some sand lances tried to escape the loons by going deeper underwater. Down deep lay the real treasure for which the fishermen had come: a fat, expensive fish normally not catchable in winter at all: the sea bream, fished beyond the inland sea in April, not January. But now, lured by the deep-diving sand lances, the sea bream rose from their hiding places. And so, lines baited with the little lances, the Japanese fishermen reaped a bounty, a fortune, of bream.

Here came a drawing of the men in their rowboat, the shoal of sand lances colliding, dancing, and breaking through the sea surface, a few diving down where the sea bream hovered. Among them, loons swam with their feet far back on their bodies like little outboard motors, some gliding underwater or plummeting with what looked like loon glee and abandon. Over the sand floor branched fishing lines, hooked and baited with the lances. This was no Picasso — had Junko drawn it herself? — but it finely portrayed a mystery of humans intertwined with nature in wordless consultation.

"Loons," writes Junko, after a description of the loons and fishers and their fishing grounds, "were worshipped as messengers from Heaven." Her story goes on to tell how fishermen built shrines edging little islands in the fishing grounds. There's a photo of one shrine where a Shinto priest and a loon fisher pray and offer rice wine and the morning's first fish. The shrine is lonely and beautiful on the stones. The fishermen, writes Junko, show affection to the birds — loons chase the best fish close to the men, so close the men "might have reached the backs of the birds."

I thought about the loon fishers all night, especially the part where loon and fisherman floated all December long in wordless communion. I thought of Aaju and the polar bear: the woman gaining the bear's trust with her song.

I began, in my bunk, to consider the word *wilderness*, and I started to realize it was a particularly English word — connected to the sensibility of Franklin, whose namesake body of water we now navigated, and to all the *Marmalados* who came before and after him. It did not seem to be a word that belonged to Japanese loon fishers, who were not separate from the loons or their place. Was there a French word for wilderness? During my time in Montreal I'd learned that English words did not always have a French counterpart. The word "happiness," for example, had been translated for me many times, but had always taken a phrase or even a paragraph. The word "naughty" was in the same boat. Now, it appeared, "wilderness" was joining the ranks. If I wanted to say, in French, "The polar bear was *in the wilderness*," how might I say it?

I thought about this for some time. I asked bilingual passengers; but it was not until later that I found, from Quebec poet and novelist Louis Hamelin, a real answer.

"Maybe you could say, not 'wilderness' — there is no word for that — you could say, 'The polar bear was in *son element.*'"

"*Son element?*"

"I think so . . ."

I liked his uncertainty. He made me see how an English tongue forced a presumptuous way of looking at the land, the loons, and the bear. By naming wilderness I was in danger of unfastening all that the Beechey Island bear and Japanese loons had tried to tell me. "The wilderness" was other, outside myself, overseen by a human world distant from it. *Son element* — "the bear's element" — wove being and element into one: air filled the bear's lungs. Earth created his body and was of one substance with him. We were not overseers gazing from a separate zone, and we laid no claim.

chapter fifteen

TRACING ONE WARM LINE

EACH NIGHT I returned to the ship's library with my skein of wool and crochet hook: I'd made headgear of handspun yarn in the ochres and golds of Gros Morne's Tablelands, one of Newfoundland's natural wonders and a site, potent and energized, to which I returned as often as I could. The yarn invited hand and spirit to work, and it also made me more attentive to fibres in the wild, more likely to notice muskox wool caught in Arctic grasses and roots. A passenger called Gwen had given me muskox wool she'd collected in Dundas Harbour: a rich brown, twigs and debris stuck in the fibres. It was pungent— there's a reason they're called muskoxen—but I liked this: months after it left the tundra the wool would hold the musky warmth of the animals.

In my journal I'd begun to tuck fragments of the land and things we encountered. There was an unspoken understanding that we shouldn't just pick up whatever took our fancy:

the land wasn't a department store or souvenir shop. There were debates. We had a little table on board where people laid stones and specimens they'd found, for the geologists and the other passengers to study and interpret. But was it right to take these objects? What about keeping stones to observe, then dropping them farther along on the journey? Did moving stones from the Boothia Uplift to the Franklinian Miogeo-syncline constitute geological interference — or even moral transgression? Some passengers restrained their collecting urges, while others' pockets bulged with sandstone and pebble conglomerate.

Why did I take a tiny fern from Dundas Harbour and press it in my journal? A piece of the land's vocabulary, a red-and-green word, but what did it say and why did I imagine taking it might let the land whisper to me forever? Seaweed I'd collected in False Strait walking with Junko had already turned to crumbs.

I turned to the muskox wool from Dundas Harbour for comfort and a sense of home. The washroom of cabin 108 had a tiny sink. I stood picking out debris, then floating the wool to disengage fragments from its oil and fibres. Leaf and seed casings stayed hopelessly caught. For a long time I picked and rinsed, trying not to block the sink with flotsam, then I drew the fibres long and free. Sunlight threaded and flashed through the sea's lace and landed on my porthole ledge, where I blotted water from the wool and laid it to finish drying — now clean and bright and so wispy I had to watch out in case it floated under the bunk or behind the cabinet where I'd stashed my licorice. I watched in case Yoko blew through our door and set it afloat. I found things to weigh it down: a hairpin, my pencil, my invitation to dine with the captain.

"Ancient *umingmak*," Bernadette Dean had written in my journal beside a wisp I had not washed, "in the land of ice and snow...bearing secrets of long ago."

Bernadette's great-grandmother, Shoofly, had made important clothing out of what animals had shared of themselves. Nathan Rogers sang, in his father's "Northwest Passage," of "tracing one warm line." How devoid of this warm line my life had felt, uprooted from ancestry, living in industrial cities and mill towns, not understanding messages from animals or from ancestors the way Bernadette and others in the North appeared to do. But wool, for me, was a kind of saviour from the cold. Wool was "one warm line" I felt in my hands; it had come from animals and it brought me a message from my own grandmother.

After we immigrated to Newfoundland, my father's mother sent me handmade clothing no Canadian child in her right mind would have worn: orange, purple, and green webs of yarn, stitched into vests. She mailed these in pillowcases covered in postage stamps and wrote letters about how her fortune-telling predictions were coming true with Mrs. Melia and the Hobbeses on her street, and how she'd soon get her senior's bus pass and could visit the swans of Morpeth. "*P.S. Your grandad found a piece of tin in his beer and he might get money from the company because he sent them a letter to complain.*"

Upon her death, decades after I realized I couldn't wear her vests in school without being tortured, I secretly claimed a striped blanket she'd made for my father. It grew old and delicate, but I used it to warm my knees while reading by the woodstove. One year, I decided to get a goat. It was an alpine goat that I believed well-suited to the woods around the house, but a friend thought otherwise. She retrieved my grand-mother's blanket, stormed outside, and wrapped it around my goat, Sally, fastening it with clothespins from my line and a few safety pins she kept in her pockets. Sally trampled the blanket through mud and thistles and tore gaping holes in its already compromised structure. Part of it scrunched around her head like a bonnet. I had to release any hope of getting it mended or cleaned. I washed and hung it on the line to see if there were salvageable sections I might make into cushions, but there were not. I made a fire in the rock pit under our birch trees and into it I lowered and burnt the last remnant I owned of my grandmother.

That same day I rummaged in my closets to find wool and wondered how to make things out of it. I made a scarf and hat set for our dog to wear to the local Santa Claus parade. In it our dog looked so dignified that when he peed on the hot dog seller's trousers she didn't suspect him. I made a hat that bore a crocheted wire birdcage and a bluebird in the cage. It was the bluebird of happiness. As long as I made things out of wool, no unhappiness could haunt me for long. Making sense of wool untangled me. I felt comfort as long as my hook was on the fly. Knowledge of how to work the wool had come enfolded in the smoke of the fire in which I'd burned my grandmother's blanket.

Now, in our ship's library, I drew tufts of clean muskox wool to their full lengths: two to four inches. I had some red wool and wanted to make a hat incorporating the raw *uming-mak* wisps.

"*What now, Grandma?*"

"*Work each bit of raw wool in like you'd do with any wool. Don't worry. It won't come loose or fall out.*"

I was tracing one warm line in the place we call the North-west Passage. I traced it with wool of ancient *umingmak* and with help from my grandmother.

Nathan sang to me while I worked on my muskox hat and wrote notes and observations on slips of paper.

"How's the new song going?" I asked.

"Still working on it." He took "The Turning" out of his pocket and unfolded it. "I'm changing it around, adding stuff. Want to hear it?"

I worked the wool as he sang the song, whose second verse went deeper into the refrain's loneliness.

A noble clipper breaks the icy tide
Safe and sound, her passengers are deep asleep inside.
But I am on her deck, the salt spray on my neck,
Fighting hard to keep the lonely agony in check
Before long she will welcome in the day.
Down below the waterline I'm safely stowed away.
Asleep within my berth, considering my worth and purpose.
Slowly fading into shades of blue and grey . . .

Making sense, making a song, a garment, a story — making all these things in the cold in the company of stones and bones . . . Nathan and I were each doing what his own father had described in song: tracing that one warm line. Everyone on the ship did this in his or her own way, and it was a delicate, human endeavour, full of possible wrong turnings and accident.

As Nathan sang I thought about the filaments of warmth leading through the heart and from one friend to another — ancient and new, delicate and immortal. I had to trust that they, like wool of the ancient *umingmak*, would hold, that they'd stay in the weave and not fall out. So much depended on patience and forgiveness: with these it was easier to bear desolation and loneliness on any voyage. In the library my soul held together with muskox wool and Nathan's songs and waves rocking over Franklin's bones, and the shaggy warmth of those ancient *umingmak* heated me through the gift of their filaments in my hands.

Alone . . . Nathan sang his new song's last line . . . *adrift upon an Arctic sea.*

He watched me while I worked the wool.

"I come from a long line of sheep stealers," I said. "We lived in the border country between England and Scotland. My ancestors followed sheep, drank from rivers, and gathered wool caught on thistles and barbed-wire fences."

"They were gleaners."

"That's why I'm so happy collecting the muskox wool around here. I think my grandmother somehow passed on our family's old connection with wool to me, when she died."

"And you're a spinner of yarns."

I wove another muskox tuft into my work and felt excited that tomorrow, when we landed at Pasley Bay, I could search the terrain for more fragments of that one warm line.

* * *

MY HIKING BOOTS looked like lobes of some mushroom cracked off the bole of an old warrior tree. I was proud of the time and distance they'd covered and imagined them someday walking around the world. My junior high swim team had called me "Chicken Wings" because I was so ineffectual, but on a slow walk I felt I could go on forever. My shipmates chose daily between two offered walks—short and long—on the tundra. I always chose the long one, scrambling rocky hills, contouring headlands, striding toward an elusive horizon with those old boots working like boots should, their cracks thirsting for the mink oil.

But at Pasley Bay I made a discovery about time and distance. To get away from the geologists I chose the short walk, and discovered it wasn't shorter than the long walk at all. It was longer and had a lot more in it.

Pasley Bay was a spot important to the white man's version of Arctic history: it was the site of a stranded ship, an icebound crew, and a sailor's gravesite marked with remnants of a burial cairn. The ship was the *St. Roch*, first vessel to traverse the Northwest Passage from both west and east. Its crew had been given multiple tasks: they were to police Inuit communities, record census data, be the first to traverse Arctic waters from a new direction, and serve as a physical and symbolic notice to the world that Canada held sovereignty here. Henry Larsen captained the ship and wintered it in Pasley Bay in 1942 on its eastbound voyage. During that winter, Albert "Frenchy" Chartrand cooked food for the sled dogs. He was boiling oats, corn, rice, tallow, and seal fat in a drum set on a couple of Primus stoves when he fell ill and later died of a heart attack. He was the only Roman Catholic on board and his shipmates wanted a priest to attend his burial, so Larsen dogsledded with a shipmate, along with Gjoa Haven Inuit guides named Ikualaaq and Kinguk, to fetch Oblate Henri Pierre from Kellett River, over 640 kilometres to the southeast. The trip took seventy-one days. Pierre held a shipboard requiem, then sprinkled snow, not holy water, over the grave. The crew built a cairn and marked the grave with a brass plate.

But little now remained. Ken McGoogan had brought a bottle to leave at the site, with a message inside documenting the story. "We think," he said, pointing, "the boat came in down there, because it's so sheltered."

The terrain stretched far, the water a meandering trail of unbroken silver with a haze that gave me the feeling we were looking through the land's memory. Ken led us to an unmoving shoreline where lay debris he said had been left there by the *St. Roch* and its crew all those years ago. Here were fragments of silvered wood, pieces of a crate possibly from the 1940s. In my sketchbook I documented a rust-eaten coffee pot, its spout elegant and extended, ready to pour Larsen's coffee. The stones and the pot shared gold and red hues; the metal and stone had for years exchanged elements and were turning into a single substance. Here we were witnessing that operation in midexchange, and I knew the Arctic had surely begun to change the way I experienced time. Events moved while appearing motionless.

I grew impatient with the story of Larsen and his crew,

however fascinating, as the tundra pulled me from the group and its air touched me, whispering of *now*, this moment, *my* presence here and not Larsen's or Frenchy Chartrand's or the oblate's. The tundra was a living presence not consecrated by any church or sprinkled with holy snow.

Was any man an agent by which snow became sacred?

I was aware of what my white-haired mystic friend, Art Andrews, had told me about similar geography at our old haunt back home, the Witless Bay Line. "I need to be out here," he said — we were near the barrens' great, erratic stones, left behind when glaciers had scoured his trout-fishing grounds — "among the non-denominational boulders."

Now, in Pasley Bay, I felt a new relationship with the ground: I looked close, and the ground sent a line of energy through my eyes and strung it through me so my body and the ground were held in tension together. I felt each step, how soft the stepping was on the red-gold hair of the earth's body. Because I'd embarked on the so-called "short walk," there wasn't the hurry there'd been on longer trails I'd taken. I'd been in such a rush to cover ground on those walks, to see the span of land and return to the ship on time, that I'd been unable to feel what I now sensed at Pasley Bay. I'd always thought I knew how to slow down. Now I sensed I'd been heeding some secret propulsion, rather than confronting my fear of stillness.

All over the tundra lay bones and fragments. I found it hard to believe that the coffee pot on the ground was from Larsen's day. I felt the same about the silvered boards. Maybe they had come from the *St. Roch*, wintering in the ice-choked bay, but who said these things hadn't belonged to Inuit hunters? As I moved from the Larsen site the ground became more and more present. Colours, tiny plants that the wind had thatched into the terrain. Then, an aberration in the weave: what looked like a twig, sticking an inch out of the plants.

This did not put itself here.

I stared, walked over for a closer look, and knelt, hesitant to touch. The stick was cylindrical, wooden with a flattened end, and protruded at a ninety-degree angle from the earth, which was strange, since nothing else here came perpendicular from the ground. Everything lay huddled and slanted against centuries of weather. There was no one else around. I took the end of the wooden piece in my fingers and gently pulled.

Out it slid like a bone loosened from its socket — smooth and old, yet containing a remnant of oil, silky and friendly to my hand: the land had articulated something human. I looked around and the only human I saw was Aaju approaching in her kilt and rubber boots. If anyone would know what this bone-like object was doing in the ground, she would. She strode toward me with her gun on her shoulder. I really liked Aaju. I liked how she thought before she spoke, and how she'd told me that in her ordinary life in Iqaluit there was a lot of work to do — the manual, daily work of living life, and thinking work as well, in her legal studies — and the work felt often unrewarded, whereas on this expedition, she said, she was treated like a queen.

I waved, hunkered on the thatched ground. Should I have removed the wooden piece? I placed it back in its hole where it looked as if I hadn't touched it — which comforted me. I didn't want to be a person who rearranged things in the North, or displaced or desecrated them.

"There's something. . ." I called. Aaju came over and bent down.

"Ah!"

"Is it a tent peg or something?"

"No, not a tent peg." She slid the piece out of its hole and held it against the sky, appreciating it and obviously recognizing it. "These are *pauktuutit*. A peg for drying caribou skin."

She was looking not at the peg now, though she still held it, but at the ground.

"What?"

"I'm looking for the others. We put five in a circle, to let the fur dry. It faces skin-up, so it can dry." She scanned the ground and found a second peg, and a third. "We do that to this day. These must be . . . the crew from that ship must have . . ."

I'd made no connection between the *pauktuutit* and the old coffee pot or the boards or any of the debris our historian said may have belonged to the *St. Roch*. Was Aaju implying that the wintering crew of the *St. Roch* had left these pegs?

"But they were European," I said.

"But they would have learned that from us," Aaju said. "Otherwise their skins would have been no good. They would have all curled up."

It appeared Aaju thought the pegs dated from that 1942 vessel. She knew a ton more about everything we encountered on our journey than I did. But I couldn't shake the question of which pieces of peg, pot, or bone belonged to white man's history and which to an ongoing life of people now living in the North. Aaju, instead, spoke the truth that these two ways of life had been intertwined for a long time. Larsen's ship might not have come unstuck had it not been for his Inuit guides Ikualaaq and Kinguuk. And where would I have been in my own reading of the North without Aaju and Bernadette, Inuit women patiently explaining their homeland to people like me, who had no intention of staying and who persisted in calling the terrain the Northwest Passage? To this day, Aaju had told me, her people hunted caribou. Mine continued hunting down the myth that a white, empty terrain awaited our "discovery."

People had approached us and now Aaju accompanied our group to a place that appeared to have nothing in it. I found myself wondering if she was ever amused by our rapt attention to everything she said. *Can't these people see?* I imagined her thinking. *Do they think there's nothing here? Or, if they do imagine there's something, why do they need to be told what it is?*

"This low vegetation all around us," she said, "we call *tingaujaq*: that which looks like pubic hair."

Everybody laughed.

"It's flammable," she said. "We use two flint stones to create a spark."

How slow I was, on the tundra, to catch Aaju's subversive humour. I try now to remember if people laughed or said anything to indicate they'd got her erotic reference, but I suspect no one did.

The *tingaujaq* was peppered with yellow flowers Aaju said would soon change and become fluffy. "Then, when we're walking, this flower reminds us, 'You have to wear a coat, you have to hunt caribou, the winter is coming.'" It was August, and in a very few weeks the sun's warmth would recede. We stepped over Arctic willow roots, silver and spiralling—Aaju said they were hundreds of years old—the willows hugging the earth, low and horizontal. We came to rocks that in any other land would be classified as low-lying, but Aaju said that here they were a height of land, full of nutrition.

"Birds shit all over the rock because they roost here, since it is a high point... though not very high ..."

Aaju stayed with this rock as people walked on. The rock was covered in orange-gold lichen, like a map on pewter-coloured skin. "I love this," she said. "I love the colours." She moved slowly around the stone, drinking in the richness of its blaze. "I wish I had my camera."

I wondered what the land told Aaju that she kept private. How generous she was, and patient. I'd seen her eat black crowberries that to me tasted like water. She found a sweetness I couldn't detect. I wondered if it was hard for her to walk with us and try to speak, on the land's behalf, to aid our perception. She spent more time than we did with the blazing rock. If the *tingaujaq* flowers spoke to her, in their small voice, of putting on a coat and hunting caribou, then what did the lichen say, with its minutiae of cascading form and its yell of colour, which to the rest of us appeared silent?

I left Aaju alone with the rock and moved to a slip of water where Junko the loon scientist beheld a flotilla of tiny hatchlings.

"Their Japanese name," she said, "is *ice duck*."

Skeins of water appeared among willows and ground-hugging leaves, reflecting the sky with a softness that made them spectral. A pond lay encircled by reeds surprisingly tall: caught between their spears hung white tufts from the *umingmak*, the muskoxen who'd stopped to drink then moved on.

Accepting gifts shouldn't be as hard as it is. A dear friend of mine, forced by circumstance to rely on people's gifts and kindness, once told me it was wrong of me to be so independent. "People need," he said, "to heal themselves by being generous. When I'm forced to accept people's generosity I tell myself it's a blessing to be able to give. You should let people do it for you. Don't be the one who is giving all the time."

I walked around the lake, collecting wisps of muskox wool, and let the earth give this gift to me. I tried not to feel guilty or undeserving. Was anyone else in need of this wool? Did anyone even know it was here? I took it, as the earth and the *umingmak* perhaps wished me to, and I washed it and am reverently using it, piece by piece, to this day.

But, maybe a bird needed it.

There is always a danger of presumption.

THAT NIGHT WE headed down the coast of King William Island, where 129 men of Franklin's 1845 expedition, forced by pack ice to abandon ship, had marched to their fabled deaths. I took my sketchbook to the library, where Sheena was giving one of her guided art workshops. In a box on the table were cards on which she had written cryptic instructions. She had turned the cards face down.

"Pick one," she said mischievously.

I gingerly shuffled around with my fingertips.

"Go on. You'll be fine."

I picked a card that said *distort something*. I looked at her for some explanation but she continued working on her own study.

I was baffled, and a little afraid. Distort something?

As I struggled over my chosen card our ship approached Rae Strait, named after John Rae, the Scottish explorer who went back to England to give Jane Franklin the unwelcome news that, not only had her husband failed to find the coveted Northwest Passage, but his crew, hallucinating as they marched, their flesh wasting in tattered silk under-vests and herringbone waistcoats, had resorted to cannibalism. It had all happened mere miles from where our ship was now positioned. This European story floated inside me and conflicted with all I had seen and felt on the land: a place so powerful and benevolent that it felt, underfoot, more sustaining and profound than anywhere I had walked in the southern world.

As we headed farther down the coast of King William Island, I was glad of the water under our ship: like my growing perception of the North's deep mystery, it possessed no straight lines, no corners, no easy, linear logic. It held, in suspension, hidden weeds intertwined with dreams and bones. If anything was distorted, I felt, as I contemplated Sheena's koan, it was my own continual attempts to map this journey instead of realizing that I was the map, and this powerful, Northern land had begun tracing itself into me.

chapter sixteen

GJOA HAVEN

THE NEXT MORNING we landed at Gjoa Haven, the only settlement on King William Island. The hamlet exemplifies the
double vision of a European history imposed on a supposed
"New World" that is, in fact, old. Like other Arctic sites, it
has both a European and an Inuit name. The *Gjøa* was the ship
of Norwegian explorer Roald Amundsen, who in 1903 stayed
there to study the magnetic pole. In the same breath, European history often credits Amundsen with founding the community yet says he stayed as long as he did so that he could
learn from the Inuit, who taught him their ancient ways. The
harbour's Inuktitut name, *Uqsuqtuuq*, refers to the plentiful fat
that nomadic hunters found in the area.

We landed by Zodiac and an Inuk named Simon approached
to help answer our questions. He wore a handmade woollen hat
whose stripes of flame, azure, and indigo blazed like the northern lights. It had an extravagant tassel of the same brilliant yarn.

"Your hat," I said. "It's beautiful wool."

"Yes."

"It's crocheted."

"I've had it ten years.'

"It looks brand new. Where did it come from?"

"I got it in northern Quebec." He turned to lead us farther into the hamlet, over sandy earth that looked raw and packed down, like ground that has been dug for a construction site then indented with machinery tracks.

"Traditionally," Bernadette Dean told me as we walked behind him, "King William Island was the place where Inuit went to hunt bear. They didn't stick around. No one lived here." They lived, she said, along Back River, located beyond a sheltered inlet quite far to the south. In the late 1920s the Hudson Bay Company had begun an outpost here, yet as late as 1960 there were no more than a hundred permanent residents, as Inuit continued their own ways of using the land, counter to the white habit of permanent, static settlement. Gjoa Haven Inuit today continue hunting, fishing, drum dancing and throat singing, but still leave the settlement—which now houses a thousand—to go back to their traditional camps in places like Back River.

Beyond Simon, watching us stumble up from the beach in our rubber boots, a child of seven carried her baby brother amauti style, bundled into the back of the men's hoodie she wore, zippered up, sleeves knotted in front of her chest to keep the bundle secure.

As we began to walk around what Amundsen allegedly called one of the finest little harbours in the world, we became, ourselves, part of an ongoing intersection between people who called the land home and those who, for reasons of money, myth, or military imagination, were just passing through. As we headed for the community centre I felt the excitement of the children and elders who'd gathered to see us. There would be drumming and dancing and a sale of local handmade goods.

We'd come here not to shop but to learn and observe, yet I felt the competitive shopper's rush — I wanted to be first inside the hall, where people had already laid out their wares on trestles and card tables. First, though, I encountered a boy in the doorway, a teenager who perhaps hadn't made the list of official craftspersons allowed to sell inside. He'd carved tiny animals of bone and strung them into necklaces, but what held me were his carving knife and stone bear. Half the size of the boy's hand, this looked like the polar bear of Beechey Island, but there was something different about it, a thing I couldn't pinpoint.

"Are you selling the bear?"

"I'm not finished it. I thought your boat was coming in tomorrow."

"So you were getting the bear ready to sell tomorrow."

He nodded, shrouded in a hoodie like my teenager at home. In his face: regret that he wouldn't sell the bear that day, mixed with trying not to care. But I liked the bear. I liked the marks it bore of the boy's hand carving: a chiselled plane, a nick, lines confident yet soft.

"Can I buy it even though it's not finished?"

He looked at me as if I was a bit subpar on the intellectual side of things.

"I mean, would you mind? I like it the way it is."

Part of me felt ashamed. Let the artist finish his work! How would I feel if someone came up to me asking for a story I'd only three-quarters finished? I'd feel it was not my best work and I wouldn't want to let it out of my possession.

"I guess. . . " He looked over his bear as if to tell it he was sorry, then handed it to me. I paid a hundredth of what others would pay his elders for completed carvings.

"Can I take a picture of you holding the bear?"

Was there no end to my crassness? I wanted to be able to look at him again, the artist, and I knew I would love the bear he'd made. But what made the bear seem odd? Something beyond its incompletion made it inconsistent with what little I knew about polar bears.

"Sure."

"What's your name?" I couldn't buy work without knowing the artist's name, but again, I felt like an idiot, a stupid tourist with no clue how to tell a good bear from an unfinished one.

"Jacob."

As he handed me his bear I sensed he was a good carver. I love works in progress, when the vision of their maker remains alive with possibility. But when I showed the bear, in the building, to one of the other passengers, he immediately gave me his recipe for fixing its shortcomings.

"When you get home," he enthused, "get a file this size" — he indicated a three-inch finger-span — "at an art store with cutting tools. And file away those cutting marks."

But the marks were what I liked. Still, I listened. It might come in handy one day to know how to finish a stone carving of my own. I could file these instructions away under other useful information I'd never get around to implementing in this lifetime, like how to spin my muskox wool into yarn using a wooden spindle, or how to make and use an emergency sundial.

"Use 180-grit sandpaper to continue smoothing," he said, "for half an hour."

I nodded.

"Wet some dry 600 sandpaper, very fine, and continue smoothing for another two hours."

He waited for me to write this down.

"Some people use wax, but I don't. The bear will become shiny without the wax."

Shiny? The bear was so far from shiny I couldn't envision it acquiring a gleam. Did he mean the bear could become glossy, like the Inuit carvings in souvenir shops near Parliament Hill? Could this pockmarked, chalky bear of Jacob's be turned into . . . but was that what I wanted?

"Then make your own carvings by preceding all these steps with acquiring your own soapstone and buying a tiny saw to begin your form. These tiny saws, you can buy them in a hardware shop."

"Thank you." I put Jacob's bear in my pocket. Erase the marks of Jacob's hands from the bear, as if they were incorrect or unwanted? Put my idea of a perfect surface on there instead? No. I remembered my father asking me to let him refinish a rough sideboard he'd found for me around Bonavista Bay.

"It's only in museums, or those idealists on *Antiques Road*

Show," he said, "that want you to leave all the old dirt and grime the way you found it after being neglected in some old woman's basement for half a century. They don't have to live with it in their kitchens."

But I'd pleaded with my father to restrain his work to cleaning the piece gently and mending a broken finial. I knew he could have made the piece look like a million dollars, but I wanted the cabinet's old stories to talk.

"I left the worn-off corner all sanded down by hands opening it through the years," he said. The piece did have a corner of its door worn like a block of butter the cat had licked. I hadn't noticed this and I appreciated that he'd seen it and left it alone, and also that he told me about it. I knew, as I put Jacob's bear in my pocket, that I wanted to leave the marks of his hands on it in the same way. But what was it about the bear that didn't seem right?

I showed it to one of our scientists. "The shape seems like a polar bear, but not quite a polar bear. There's something else. It's white, but—"

"We've entered the geographical zone where the polar bear gives way to the grizzly," he said. "For a long time we thought there was no such thing as a cross between those two bears. But now, with Arctic ice melting and habitat changing for both species, people have seen hybrid bears. We've quite a bit of evidence that they're out there, and they would be in this area if they're out there at all. So maybe"—he held the bear up and examined it—"the bear you've got here is one of those. See, look. That snout, the breadth of the chest, the size of his head . . ."

So it appeared the bear was, in more ways than one, in a process of becoming.

I went into the community hall for the dancing. Around one side sat men, women, and children of Gjoa Haven who'd made things to sell. A child in a magnificent duffle coat decorated with embroidery and beads and the tail of a wolf or a fox wove in and out of the vendors, and Elisabeth of the exquisite woollen underwear said to me, "If only I had a coat like that, big enough to fit me. . . " The coat had puffed shoulders and bell sleeves, and it had an extra skirt or two so it was less like any kind of coat I'd ever seen and more like a ceremonial dress made for the cold North.

"I'll ask her."

"You will?"

"There she is now, running into the washroom. I'll go ask her."

"You won't follow her?"

"Sure. I'll go in and ask her who made the coat."

I ran after the child and gave her what I hoped was a not-too-frightening smile. "Hi."

"Hi." Giggles.

"My friend Elisabeth loves your coat. She wondered who made it."

I followed the girl around vendors of bear-claw necklaces and carvings finished with the appropriate tools until they gleamed, through moccasins and hats, to a woman standing talking to friends. Elisabeth tentatively came over, and the next time I spoke to her she held a diagram on which she and the maker had agreed upon every detail of a coat that would turn out, in months to come when the maker mailed it to Elisabeth's home in the south, to be so ceremonial and magnificent it would take every ounce of Elisabeth's courage to wear it outside. Between her Gjoa Haven coat and her woollen undergarment, Elisabeth was becoming a queen of the north.

An American passenger haggled over bear-claw necklaces — grizzlies — only to find out he couldn't by law bring them into the U.S., and I wondered again about how we take unto ourselves the things that attract us. It made me think about the difference between using animal parts, such as claws, if you lived in the Arctic and if you did not. I bought two of the claws the American had relinquished. I found it strange that I could bring them to my southern part of Canada, which by now felt as distant from the North as Florida or Texas.

An old woman sat among tools and kitchen implements. She had a homemade ulu.

"It looks old." I picked it up.

She nodded.

"Did you make it?"

Nod.

There were ulus everywhere in the North, embroidered on coats and blankets and employed in people's hands, but those available to visitors were usually decorative and not made for real use. Some looked hastily made out of new materials and weren't big or strong enough for cutting anything. Aaju Peter had a real ulu with which she'd shown us how to cut raw seal meat into little squares like quivering rubies. Hers was a rolling cut, using the semi-circular blade in a rocking motion while grasping the bone handle. A real ulu had a shape beautiful to hold and look at, a beauty that came from its efficient utility and spare elegance.

"How much?"

I'd pocketed Jacob's bear and two grizzly claws, and here I was coveting the ulu. It bothered me that it was well used and that the woman might have nabbed it from her kitchen as a last thought before coming to where we'd gathered. Take an old woman's ulu away? I should bloody well use my own knives with their Sheffield steel and ivory-coloured handles, one for the marmalade and another for butter from a Devonshire cow.

"Sixty dollars."

What is this business of wanting, needing to take a little piece of something, some place, or someone, to own it and make it become part of us? The polar bear had spoken to me about the reality of oneness, but here in the community hall at Gjoa Haven I became separate again, separate and wanting to be part of ulu, part of grizzly, part of Jacob's bear, and part of the dance now forming on one side of the arena. But I couldn't become part of the dance, much as I love dancing and have always danced, making a fool of myself on the street. I'd done something to my Achilles tendons and feared they might snap if I danced, and I had no wish to leave the north in a rescue helicopter or test my insurance company's remote assistance clause.

I bought the ulu. Like a rainbow, its blade was a section of circle whose span was only partly visible. Perhaps that circle, and the wholeness spoken by the land, the polar bear, and the muskoxen, existed despite my intermittent separation from it. I held the ulu — its brass shaft and bone handle and steel blade so lovely — and tried not to feel I'd stolen it from the woman who'd made it. Had I not happily sold many things I'd made? Belts, bags, hats, and stories. I'd sold many important parts of myself, and my own creations, and with the proceeds had bought meat, apples, plane tickets, and potatoes. We make and love a thing and sell it, and maybe women do this more — sell what we've made, used, and loved — and maybe we're in it together, the business of creating, parting with, losing, yearning, failing, and trying to become whole.

Jacob — the boy who'd carved the bear. The woman whose ulu I now held — her name was Sarah. I knew both their names because I'd asked. But they neither knew nor asked to know mine.

WHILE THE DANCING went on, a few of us walked to the community office to look at artifacts from Gjoa Haven's history. I gravitated to a quiet corner and let others look at carvings and charts, but someone followed me: a Gjoa Haven man I'd not noticed before. I wore my husband's ancient, gargantuan Helly Hansen raincoat with cement and paint and duct tape all over it, and I knew that compared with other passengers I looked scruffy. Later my husband would say the jacket must have been the reason this man chose to tell me what he did. It was a jacket, my husband said, that invited revelation.

"How long" — the man spoke close to my ear — "are you going to be around?"

"I think we're just here for the day."

"Too bad you won't be around next week."

When intriguing interactions come my way I have some mechanism that prompts me to answer as if everything is perfectly normal. This is sometimes bad, but in this case I figured I was too old and shabbily dressed to be the object of either flirtation or robbery. The man, very close, spoke in an undertone, but I detected no danger.

"Why's that, now?"

"About sixty years ago, Father Henry got ahold of Franklin's logbook."

"Father Henry?"

"The priest here. An old Inuk guy handed the documents to the priest. He wrapped them in a canvas material that had wax in it, then a metal container, then buried it here in Gjoa Haven."

"Franklin's logbook?"

It was pretty hard not to get a bit excited at the mention of such a document. I remembered a tiny notice taped to the wall in a cheap hotel during my sojourn in Paris in my twenties. It said, in French, that no matter how wild the flames, in the event of fire or any other unwanted excitement, hotel guests were entreated to maintain their *sang froid*. The logbook of Lord Franklin had never been found. Not a button from his garment had been reclaimed. Everyone on board our ship had at some time on this journey entertained dreams of Franklin's this and Franklin's that showing up before our eyes on the tundra or in the waters lapping the rocks. Nathan Rogers had fasted during much of the journey, and I'd been sending psychological soundings of my own into the land, air, and waters around our vessel. We were all constantly listening for clues to this mysterious land. Franklin's logbook? Was the man raving? Had I heard him right?

"Right here in the town. Next week we will excavate it."

"Really."

"Only one uncle was aware of it and he kept it secret until last year. He was the one who kept the secret."

"Your uncle?"

"We have an archaeologist coming next week with an assistant. The excavation will be properly monitored, and we'll send the document down to Ottawa to be examined."

"Ottawa?"

"There is a lot of legal stuff. If you want to come into my office I can show you all the confidential documents."

I followed him. He took papers from a desk and started photocopying and handing the copies to me. There was a contract between the man's family and some barristers and solicitors in Sherwood Park, Alberta. He also gave me a report of a meeting his family had held with representatives from the Nunavut government, a historian, and legal counsel regarding the buried documents believed to be related to the 1845 lost Franklin expedition.

The report talked about documents wrapped in waxed fabric and put in a tin that was then buried. There would indeed be an excavation this month, said the report, and the tin would go, unopened, to the Canadian Conservation Institute in Ottawa. The family agreed the papers had to be properly conserved, but they were adamant that in the end such a historical find had to come back to Gjoa Haven. There was talk of custody agreements, temporary and permanent: who would control the Franklin papers, and who would really own them, once they came out of the ground? The family members had signed a sheaf of consent forms outlining how they did or did not want this preliminary report used, and the man put these in my hands as well.

"Why are you giving me this?"

"We've been waiting for the right time. The government is trying to focus more on the Northwest Passage. They want to do something other than just monitor it. And now the timing is right."

I heard music floating from the dance down the road, and cheers from the soccer game nearby. The other stragglers who'd come into this building with me to see the display of artifacts had gone off to where the fun was. I was alone with this man and his Franklin logbook story, and my heart pounded. It reminded me of my first reporting job at the *Evening Telegram* in St. John's after I'd graduated from journalism school. They gave me tame assignments veteran reporters didn't want: Red Cross blood donor clinic schedules and Rotary luncheons. The highlight of my reporting day was when the sports editor got up from his seat every morning at 11:15, opened our third-floor fire escape door, and clapped his hands to send a thousand starlings flying off the branches of a couple of old ash trees struggling for survival in the courtyard. This was before computers: we had IBM Selectric typewriters and there was a printing press that took up the whole second floor. News came in on teletype machines in a cubicle whose floor was covered in an unending tongue of paper printed with intelligence from Reuters and the Canadian Press, most of it trivial.

But about a month after I'd been hired, I was in the news-room alone. Everyone had gone for lunch and I was taking that opportunity to continue surreptitious work on my novel when suddenly alarms began to clang, hoot, and buzz in the teletype area. I remember keeping my *sang froid*, though any-one with a grain of sense would've jumped up to see what was the matter. But I was writing a novel.

"The waters of his emotion receded from what he had believed to be his heart," I wrote, "and left behind a bed of jut-ting shale. . . " or some such nonsense. The teletype machines were shaking up and down. Why was there no other journalist in the entire building? Not even Regina Best, who wrote one weekly column about society dinners yet was always wafting around the newsroom in a glorious caftan as if she were indis-pensable at all times. I supposed I'd better get up and have a look.

I ventured among the teletypes and picked up one of the paper ribbons, now strewn ankle-deep.

The Pope.

I didn't care about the Pope, but a lot of people did, and it appeared he had been shot.

What a nuisance. I knew from the movies that I was sup-posed to run like the wind to the second floor, flailing my arms and yelling, "Stop the presses!"

Printers and apprentices would come out from behind the machinery in their green visors, pencils behind their ears, Orson Welles among them as William Randolph Hearst. And he'd fire me, that's what he'd do, for daring to stop the presses when anyone could see the Pope hadn't been shot at all, it was just my imagination. I went back to my desk and sat paralyzed until the real journalists came back from their lunches and sprang into action.

What were they teaching in journalism school these days? Hadn't the senior journalists always said journalism school was a joke? Hadn't I known it myself, the year I passed television reporting class by being the person who drew rain and clouds for the weather forecaster's graphics, while the likes of Susan Ormiston were out grinding the heads of lying, thieving politicians into the dirt and making the truth about everything come out of hiding? Which was why Susan Ormiston was now the Canadian national newscast's star correspondent, now in a hijab, now in a camouflage helmet, bullets whizzing past her face, while I — where was I?

I was in Gjoa Haven, listening to a man called Wally Porter tell me he knew where the lost logbook of Sir John Franklin lay buried in the ground. This I cared about, not like the Pope, and what was more, a lot of other people cared too...maybe not as many as cared about the Pope, but still...I couldn't allow paralysis to overtake me here. I had to do something. Where was a pay phone when you needed one? Why had I neither kept my old Rolodex full of important phone numbers nor joined the twenty-first century and bought a smartphone? How was I going to stop the presses this time? The Franklin logbook, to be unearthed in mere days, here in Gjoa Haven, after more than 160 years, containing secrets of glory and ignominy, scurvy and cannibalism, in Franklin's own words...

Wally Porter had revealed all he was going to tell me. He had to go and do paperwork, he said, to get ready for the big day. I held his secret papers and decided I was not going to be the journalist who broke this story; I didn't have it in me. I had, throughout this journey, been on a search that included white explorers' artifacts; but I did not specialize in them. I kept thinking about the muskoxen, the land, and the Beechey Island bear, whose eloquence was my real headline, my personal focus of study. I didn't have the confidence, the passion for a byline, or any stake in the Great White Explorer theme of Arctic history. But I knew someone who did.

"Have you seen," I called, racing through Gjoa Haven asking passengers snapping photos or strolling from the soccer game to the dance hall, "our Arctic historian, Ken McGoogan?"

Someone pointed to the Co-op Store.

I ran up the steps and down aisles of tinned corned beef and green peppers flown in, like myself, from another universe, my heart pounding ridiculously. There stood Ken beside the tea bags. I tapped his shoulder, knowing I was about to tell him something akin to telling Sir Galahad I'd spied a piece of silver chalice sticking out of the ground, a drop of divine grace clinging to its rim.

"Would you mind" — I was breathless — "coming outside? I have something I want to tell you."

Ken followed me to the stoop and leaned against the wall while I told him the story. He listened extremely well, neither showing excitement nor interrupting what must have seemed a completely wild and unbelievable story. The more I talked, the more I wished he'd say something, but he let me go on until I was finished.

"He's in that building," I finally nodded toward the community office. "At least he was a few minutes ago."

I had an idea Wally Porter might vanish, whereupon Ken would have every right to think I'd made him up. I already felt a bit suspect in the eyes of our shipboard experts since I tended to doze off if they went on too long about alluvial sediments or whether a skua was pomarine or parasitic, whereas I could sit crocheting in the library until all hours listening to Nathan Rogers sing "Dark Eyed Molly." The fate of Franklin, though, interested me almost as much as it did Ken, and as I told him about the buried logbook I knew my face was burning and wild. Ken would have done well in a Parisian hotel fire. Throughout my breathless exposition he held fast to his *sang froid*. He calmly followed my directions, found Wally Porter, listened to him as carefully as he had listened to me, and filed a news story that eventually led to national and international headlines.

That night at dinner our table shared a bottle of scotch. I felt happy that Ken had been able to do the story better justice than I would have done, knowing in his heart and in every vein all the historical detail forming the context of the events, and having the journalistic contacts to get the story out. But I was still a tiny bit proud of myself for being the conduit through which the story had decided to flow, and at dinner I felt it was time, finally, to wear my crocheted explorer's beard, attached snugly and effectively to the face by way of discreet loops around one's ears. I'm sure the beard did a lot to cement my reputation, among the ship's scholars, as a true finder of important Arctic secrets.

chapter seventeen

JENNY LIND ISLAND
AND BATHURST INLET

OVERNIGHT OUR SHIP navigated the channel south of King
William Island, crossing the imaginary line where Rae Strait
becomes Queen Maud Gulf. By early morning we'd anchored
off small, misty Jenny Lind Island, and by Zodiac landed on
its sandy shores. The little island is named not after any naval
officer or secretary to the admiralty, but after a soprano whom
Scottish Arctic explorer John Rae had admired in London, a
woman known as the "Swedish Nightingale." People called a
lot of sopranos nightingales in the nineteenth century—I'd
stood on another island, Twillingate in Newfoundland, birthplace of soprano Georgina Stirling or "Marie Toulinguet,"
who became known as the "Nightingale of the North." Jenny's
and Georgina's islands were foggy and remote outcrops as
far as fashionable European concert-goers were concerned,
and neither had ever been visited by a real nightingale, a bird

Europeans lent a literary romanticism not unlike their notions of alluring treasure in the colonies. Bernadette Dean was having none of it.

She and I walked in fog on Jenny Lind Island — once more I'd foregone the long walk and was slowly taking the short one, reading the calligraphy of snow geese footprints in the sand. Bernadette was now missing her home, especially the berry bushes. We were nearing a place where she hoped there would be blueberries, and she was lonely in a way only someone who loves her homeland can be. I didn't know that kind of loneliness, but I could see how real it was to Bernadette. Passengers on the long walk had attained height on a distant ridge, and in the fog we could barely see them. No colours shouted from their usual array of red and blue anoraks — they were blue-grey shadows walking single-file over the ridge, bent against the mist, heading away until fog swallowed the first, the second, the third . . .

"They look," said Bernadette drily, "like Franklin's men."

They did. They looked exactly like Franklin's men enacting a scene from the European imagination — and, it appeared, from the Inuit imagination as well — a scene of doomed white explorers, individuality sucked out of them by the elements, walking into oblivion.

We watched them disappear into the fog. I wondered if Bernadette saw all of us who came here, passing through, as Franklin's men; passage-navigators seeking and moving slowly, endlessly, from one end of the land to the other, never finding a centre because the centre requires us to find a point of stillness.

Through the milky fog bloomed white beings — snow geese — that appeared and dissolved in the mist, big and luminous, contracting into orbs then flinging their feathers into resplendent fans. I found two crescent-shaped bones lying on the sand mirroring each other, flat with intriguing holes and ridges, each about the size of the crescent I could make with thumb and forefinger. I hesitated, guilty, but slipped them in my pocket anyway, pieces of whiteness from the white fog. I wondered if they might be jawbones of a small Arctic fox.

Our marine biologist was walking close by. "Seal?" he said, when I showed him the bones. I did not think he sounded sure. I'd seen many seals in Newfoundland, and these bones seemed different.

"I keep thinking of a little fox every time I look at them."

"No. The molars are too small. I think what you have there is seal."

Stones loomed out of the fog: mystic columns topped by a torso and head to form a human body. I'd come to one of those stone sentinels we've learned to call inukshuks. This one was magnificent. Much taller than I, it stood trying to talk to me, one of its legs planted in sand, the other touching water. I wondered how long it had been here. I tried to imagine its stones having withstood the piling and crashing of ice on this shoreline through the past winter and spring, but I couldn't. Another scientist from our ship now appeared through the mist.

"That's a beauty," he marvelled.

"How long do you think it's been here?"

"It's hard to say."

"I mean, do you think one of our shipmates might have

built it this morning?"

"Why would you think that?" He looked at me in genuine surprise.

This was not the first time the age, provenance, authenticity, and identity of a found object had mystified us in the North and caused us to have different conjectures. The place invited multiple versions of every story we encountered. Was Franklin still floating under the water or not? Did I have seal jawbones in my pocket or bones of another animal? Was my bear polar or grizzly, or an amalgam some believed to be a mythic creation? And if the bear was a hybrid, was this old news or a new part of the long, ancient story that made up the Arctic world?

"I thought the water, the sand . . . things shift over time. Is it possible this has been here very long?"

"It could have been here for a very long time indeed."

When I got back on the ship I kept thinking about the inukshuk. Nathan sat tuning his guitar and in a flash I knew—

"*You* built it."

"What?"

"It's a beauty. People think those stones were put there a long time ago."

"Heh."

"Scientific people. They think it may have stood there for eons."

He threw his head back and his tongue piercing glinted.

"It sure is a beauty."

"Thanks, dude. How did you know?"

"Some of the stones that weren't touching the water, they were wet."

We snorted with laughter and he began practicing "Willie O Winsbury" for his performance later that night.

I was feeling sad that our journey would soon be over. Aaju and Bernadette, Nathan and Sheena and Elisabeth and others on board had made me aware of how endearing people can become even to someone who imagines she likes being alone. We'd been given notices: "Today is the last day to send your laundry." Laundry? I had no laundry—but I knew the notices meant we'd soon sail through Coronation Gulf toward our original destination of Kugluktuk, the final point before we were to disperse and return to our southern homes.

"The elders," Aaju said at dinner, "teach that the mind is so strong that—in comparison—the body is a feather blown across the tundra."

I could easily imagine myself being blown like that feather across the land we'd travelled, but I did not feel my mind was stronger than the feather. I felt lonely knowing all the souls and all the beauty I had encountered would soon disperse. That night in the lounge Nathan played and I drank brandy with the captain, with whom I'd not spoken since Wally Porter had told me of the buried canister to be unearthed in Gjoa Haven. I asked, somewhat breathlessly, what the captain thought of the canister.

"We do not know what, if anything, has been buried there," he said with utmost calm. "Franklin's logbook? I heard it, but it is a rumour. I'll believe it when I see it."

Nathan was singing "Willie O Winsbury": *Cast off, cast*

off your berry-brown gown. Stand naked on the stone... It is hard
to listen to two beautiful men at once. I was thinking how the
captain and John Franklin had known similar lines of work
and I wanted to know specifics our captain might tell me.
Meanwhile Nathan sang of captains and kings and filial and
other love through the ages, and his voice was a voice you
hear with the bones in your whole body, not just the shell like
bones in your ears.

"What kind of detail," I asked, "do you think such a logbook would have in it?"

The captain remained silent.

"What would it contain if you were writing it?"

Was it with a lord or a duke or a knight, sang Nathan, *or a
man of birth and fame*... The song was one I'd known a long
time and it had a melody that filled me with melancholy.

"They would keep writing"—the captain took a sip of
brandy, his eyes far away—"until they drew their last breath.
They would never give up."

I became aware, looking at his expression, of how easy it
was for a captain to lose his ship. I remembered that less than
four years before, the sister ship of our own had struck Antarctic ice and sunk. I asked our captain about it now.

"Yes, the captain of that ship is a friend of mine. I have
sailed that ship myself."

I saw that thinking about the lost sister ship saddened him.

He was clad all in the red silk, Nathan sang, *his hair was like
thick bands of gold*...

"What would you say," I asked, "is the most important
quality the captain of a ship should possess?"

I thought the captain might silently ponder this but he answered in a heartbeat.

"Patience."

"Patience?"

I might have imagined he'd say a captain needed presence of mind, or an ability to remain unruffled. The man sitting beside me struck me as calculating, determined, logical. But patient? Why did a captain need patience? For what might he possibly be waiting? Clearly I knew nothing about his work.

Nathan began one of his own songs, "Jewel of Paris": *There were rough seas and rain on the day that I came to the New World...*

"Yes," the captain said, remembering. "Patience."

Neither of us knew how much patience he would soon need.

ALL SEEMED TRANQUIL through the night. The moon was nearly full, pulling us toward land that had assumed a softness and a gentle allure I hadn't known the Far North possessed. In the morning we walked onto land so welcoming, yet uninhabited, it reminded me of Boyd's Cove in the Bay of Exploits in Newfoundland, where artist Gerald Squires had a vision that led him to create his great sculpture of Beothuk woman Shanawdithit. I remember when I first visited her—alone in the light and shadow of spruce and birches—and in the rocks and water all around I felt her people: the Beothuk race destroyed in Newfoundland after white men came. There is nothing bygone about the way Boyd's Cove invites human beings to a life of joy, and this same welcome, a benevolent and nourishing lay of the land, was immediately apparent in Bathurst Inlet, though no one greeted us.

I walked with Aaju and our anthropologist, Kenneth Lister, and we stopped many times at the sheer invitation of the land, in absolute certainty that people had known and loved this place and been sheltered by it. Here rose a hill, there rested a hollow, and here stood small but sheltering trees just crowded enough to soften the wind.

A solitary tree stood over a stone half-buried like a tablet in an old graveyard. It had to be the improvised gravestone of someone—but whom?

"It looks," Aaju said, "like white men's graves. Inuit graves would have had stones piled on top, unless it was the burial of an evil person."

"Thule people would have loved it here," said Kenneth. "But white men, whalers, they'd have come here for beluga. There are lots of lookouts and a beautiful beach."

Our itinerary said this place had been home to the Kingaunmiut people, who'd left remnants of stone tent rings and evidence of animals hunted for meat and skins. Even Franklin had come here—in the summer of 1821, during his first attempt to find the elusive passage. Again on this journey we found ourselves at a central point whose rays of influence spanned worlds and turned the so-called Old World Man of Europe into newcomer, visitor, writer of footnotes in the margins of a story begun long before his entrance. Though ancient, the land spoke to us of now, of its own immediate presence, an aliveness insistent and ongoing, and we were part of it. Much as I realized we were passing through as Franklin had done almost two centuries before, I felt the land say I shouldn't worry about not belonging. This land, as Aaju and Bernadette had tried to explain to me, did not judge people. It treated everyone with the same dignity, and it was up to us to show a reciprocal respect. The earth here in the North, as elsewhere in our world, depended on us to notice this.

I picked up a large feather that Richard Knapton, our ornithologist, said had belonged to a rough-legged hawk. A stone on the beach called to my hand to hold it.

"What might this be?" I asked, interrupting Marc St-Onge as he was jumping onto a boulder, getting ready to explain it to a circle of students far worthier than me. He always managed to be courteous even to the most undeserving.

"That," he said, "is sandstone and mudstone, a younger rock, only sixteen hundred million years old. It tells the story of the Bathurst fault line, which is the reason Bathurst Inlet exists."

I kept the feather and the stone. The feather had flown over the land for a fleeting time, and the stone, young as it was in the world of stones, filled me with its wordless knowledge when I held it, dark red and hard like a piece of gizzard or heart.

I stood with Kenneth Lister on the high promontory over Bathurst Inlet's beach, both of us reluctant to leave a place telling us so plainly that it had been made for people, that places can long for company just as we do. It was seductive, that beach with its mounds and hollows. I saw why Franklin had come here in a birch bark boat before his final journey, and I wondered who was buried under that European slab.

"This kind of place," Kenneth said, "is the real story, for me...a place where cultures move out of labelled territory and interact with each other, and create uncharted territory that we have not labelled...an *alive* area."

That night I went alone on deck to look at a spectacular moon, full and illuminating the Arctic landscape all by itself—mile upon mile of mercurial silver and blue enchantment. When Marc later crossed my path I asked if he'd noticed it. Marc had chipped away at my resistance to his subject. John Houston had called him a rock evangelist, and I had to agree he had the insistent conviction I'd seen among some of the religious people my first husband had known. There was something about Marc's lessons that wouldn't go away no matter how I tried to evade it. I found his teachings exasperating, yet expansive.

"Yes," he answered me, "I saw the moon, directly above the columnar jointing."

"Columnar jointing?"

"Yes, you see . . ." and any further mention of the boring old moon was lost in his excitement. Columnar jointing was a "cooling feature". . . something about thick lava flows...surfaces...sills. Something, I didn't catch what exactly, was always perpendicular to the cooling surface. Something else was hexagonal when seen from the top . . .

I'd been unable to follow his teachings in Bathurst Inlet about the Paleoproterozoic Goulburn Supergroup. I could tune in when he mentioned chaotic masses and sliding or thumping mud, but only for a moment. Geologists, I felt sure, would reduce any talk of the moon itself to the kind of rock of which it was composed, and I wasn't interested in lumps of stone for their own sake, or I imagined I wasn't.

Yet, through Marc, I was becoming aware that stone had outlived everything else that mattered to us on our route. Stone preceded life as we knew it. It preceded the polar bear on Beechey Island. According to Marc, the stone had *caused* the polar bear, since it had made possible the mineral life that fed flora that fed creatures that fed the bear. Stone lay beneath us, rose up, and had been the primary agent of change and would continue to be so whether or not I recognized it during my life—a life fleeting as a feather, according to Aaju. Rock caught my attention against my will. The red stone I'd found in Bathurst Inlet was young, Marc said—only sixteen hundred million years—nothing compared to the strange, spiral-carved rocks and fossils we saw next called stromatolites: the oldest record of life on earth, Marc said, and "ancestors to all life forms on earth today." Their spirals reminded me of a friend who'd said, when I told her I felt stuck in a rut, that what appear as closed circles can be coils of a spiral opening out in a pattern of growth.

chapter eighteen

SUPREMACY OF ROCK

ON DAY FOURTEEN of our journey, there was a shifting atmosphere on board. I thought of my husband and daughters in Montreal, harvesting figs and tomatoes and cycling down bike paths overhung with end-of-summer leaves. We were all thinking about home. Nathan Rogers missed his wife and daughter, and kept talking about how he wanted badly to see them again. Bernadette missed her blueberry grounds and longed for news of her new grandbaby.

Our itinerary told us we had one more night on the vessel before reaching our destination of Kugluktuk. At four we were to gather in the lounge to recap and share stories of the voyage, then after dinner there'd be a variety show — one of those opportunities for us all to temporarily close the door to profound thinking and open the gate to mayhem and foolishness and the kind of camaraderie I was unused to and was beginning to enjoy. Milling about in the corridors we were laughing and thinking about having a glass of scotch and finding ways to say goodbye.

"We don't say goodbye," said Bernadette Dean. "We say…" and she spoke an Inuktitut word that I didn't write down or remember.

My notes had long since spilled beyond my journal and were crammed inside a Ziploc sandwich bag, stowed in cabin 108's bedside table along with my stash of licorice pipes and chili-lime salted nuts. The Ziploc bag bulged: my journal had finally felt too official and cumbersome to take on our treks over the tundra, and the land had made it almost impossible to write notes as I walked—it said too much, and said it wordlessly. So I'd scrawled notes on random scraps—the back of our list of what to bring on the voyage, margins around our sheet bearing the names and fields of expertise of the resource staff, blank ends of the itinerary sheets slid under our cabin doors. I'd ripped pages from the notebooks Sheena McGoogan had given me and had scribbled English, Latin, and Inuktitut names of tundra flowers—nodding campion, *pulluliujuit*, *Silene uralensis*—in the old, human attempt—always of questionable success—to understand a thing by naming it. I'd written, *Everyone is looking for the red-throated loon.* I'd scrawled, *The fate of Franklin.* I had an envelope on which I'd printed *Gavia stellata*, whose feather I must have tucked inside, but the wind had blown it away. I'd folded the sheet Nathan Rogers had given me, bearing the lines of the new song he'd written on the voyage. I had my drawing of Elisabeth's woollen undergarment and the story of Emily Carr's milk bill. In my Ziploc bag I kept all these ephemera from the journey, precious to me yet insubstantial — how would I ever understand what was implied by the small things I'd managed to note or sketch? It was impossible, but these little things, and memory, and inscriptions the Arctic makes on the heart — these were all I had.

I continued to the party assembling in the lounge. I came to the area around the stairwell leading up to the captain's quarters, the space housing our table of stones and specimens: the skull of a fox Aaju had brought from Jenny Lind Island; bits of feather, bone, and botanical curiosities found and shared for discussion. On the wall hung the Royal Canadian Geographical Society's New Century Map of Canada, on which we'd daily marked the line of our journey: from Greenland through Lancaster Sound, down Peel Sound, down Franklin and Ross Straits, around King William Island and through Queen Maud Gulf past Cambridge Bay, in and out of intoxicating Bathurst Inlet, and into Coronation Gulf where our ship now headed into its last stretch bound for —

The ship lurched.

It crunched on something big, not like one of the small pieces of ice we'd scraped in Karrat Fjord. This sound kept going: a dreadful, deep displacement of our vessel out of the water, out of her gliding movement, nowhere close to any of the rocking, all smooth and rolling, we'd known before. This was some kind of rupture — the ship crashed, tilted, and tried to grind to a halt in the middle of the water but could not. Forward it juddered, and I stopped — everyone stopped. I pressed my back against the staircase and slid down to sit on the floor with my back against the most stable perpendicular surface, though it was neither perpendicular nor stable. Time did strange somersaults, as it will do when a long, smooth journey halts in a catastrophic collision. What we were experiencing was the grounding of our vessel, and while part of my brain hoped for a miraculous resolution, I began — we all began — to realize that the ship would not right itself. Something had happened to change all our plans. The ship was not going to make it to our destination.

In that eternal moment of the grinding, with its awful noise, and the beginning of the alarm siren we'd heard early in the voyage during our mandatory evacuation drill, I remembered my husband and daughters at home, and realized we might be about to sink and be lost and I'd not written a will — how foolish had I been, how stupidly unaware of the imminent mortality that dogs us all! I thought of how many years my youngest daughter had to go before she was done high school and I wondered if she could become independent without my final years of mothering.

The alarm kept insisting — the ship's engine was now silent. I looked out and saw land about a mile away, and thought perhaps we would not die after all — we had lifeboats and the land was not far off. I thought of fires on the tundra, of fishing for our food until help came — would help arrive? Or would the ship — perched aloft at a tilt of several degrees — topple and sink as its sister ship had done less than four years earlier in the Antarctic sea? What had our captain told me about such an event? What had he said, only the night before, when I asked him the most important attribute a sea captain must possess? *Patience.* I remembered not having understood that patience was what a captain needed — what our captain needed — and he needed it now, really needed it, not hypothetically.

Nathan sat beside me. I began to realize others had collected themselves, had realized we were not sinking.

"Are you okay?" Nathan was calm. I remembered that earlier on the voyage, when he'd spoken of the death of his father, he'd also told me he knew no fear of flying, since what were the chances of both himself and his father dying in plane crashes? He'd said nothing about shipwrecks, but had told me what he'd do if he did find himself in a doomed plane or in any other life-threatening situation.

"I would want to go down the way my father did," he'd said. "Giving a hand to other passengers. Making sure as many lived as possible. Trying to make them not be scared. Risking my life to save theirs. That's what my father did, and that's what I hope I would do."

The alarm kept sounding, a most insistent and terrifying reminder that we had to do something — there was a protocol and we'd been shown it during those carefree, early moments on the voyage in which an alarm drill seemed fictional, if slightly disturbing, sounding in the gulf between oneself and a remote chance of disaster — a gulf we hoped never to have to traverse.

We had to go to our cabins and get our life jackets, then come back upstairs to our muster stations, wearing the jackets, while the lifeboats were lowered.

I ran down, grabbed my life jacket, and also grabbed my Ziploc baggie full of notes — I was not going to let any sinking ship separate me from those. I zipped the bag, stuffed it in my pocket, and grabbed Yoko's laptop in case she had irreplaceable notes of her own stored in it. The door next to our cabin, the one mysteriously ajar and painted with the letters WTD that I had not comprehended, was now shut, and the initials' meaning flashed in my mind as if the words were suddenly emblazoned in full: WATER-TIGHT DOOR. That door was now — less than two feet from my cabin — presumably doing the job for which it had been designed. Up I ran to my muster station — the alarm pulsed on and on and on, invading my veins and becoming part of my heartbeat. It was like a foghorn that had strapped on shield and helmet and become warlike, waking even sailors who'd long died; a grave and deafening noise to impress upon us the dire need for right action in every detail.

Our lifeboat was lowered. We waited. Other lifeboats were now bobbing on the water, small and orange like cheerful corks, strangely jaunty. Someone said we were not necessarily going to board them – they were standing by, in case. We could see the rock on which we'd become grounded — a flat sill not deep at all. But how stable was the sill and how deep was the water around it?

People gathered, relayed information — to me it was all hearsay. I wanted someone to give me definitive comfort: were we to sink or not sink? It appeared not, but how had everyone decided this? The next hours were a lesson to me in how much more precarious I find the world than others seem to find it. In the hour after our grounding the consensus was that we were not in immediate danger. There were no vessels standing by but there might be tugboats, and we were making contact with the Canadian Coast Guard. People took their life jackets off and slung them on chairs in the lounge, but I did not remove mine. Kind passengers with sailing experience gently coaxed me, saying it was all right to take mine off, but I kept it on: we were askew on a rock, and who knew when a wind might spring up and tilt our vessel so it might slide into the gulf? Who knew how damaged our hull was?

Even when official word came from our expedition leader, over the loudspeaker, that we could take off our life jackets, I kept mine close, whereas others placed theirs back in their cabins. There would be dinner as usual, it was announced, in the dining room: late, perhaps, but delicious as always.

I watched the others file into the dining room and saw the kitchen crew carrying beautiful trays to the tables, now tilted at our new angle. Why did the sense of relief flooding the whole group not extend to me? How, I marvelled, could anyone eat a five-course dinner now? I sat on a couch in the bar near the dining room, my life jacket at my feet and my Ziploc bag of notes stuffed in my pocket, and watched people pass. How was it they were hungry? I felt I might never be able to eat again.

People were kind to me. One of the passengers, a sweet young woman who'd become a friend, offered me one of her husband's tiny sedative pills, which he'd brought on the journey "just in case." Maybe that was it. Maybe I was the only one who had not brought Lorazepam.

Sheena McGoogan, ever kind, came out of the dining room when she saw I was not unwrapping my habitual pat of Danish butter. She brought me a piece of bread, saying, "Here, I know you don't want to eat anything now, but you should have something small, even if it's only this piece of bread, because later tonight you'll wish you had eaten something." I especially loved her at that moment, and ate the bread like a child obeying a kind teacher. I remembered my concertina down in the cabin and brought it upstairs and sat with it on my lap while the others continued to eat. Night fell and everyone went to their cabins. The ship, marooned, motionless, had lost her rocking, womblike powers. I lay on the window seat in the lounge and fell asleep.

THE EARLY RISERS came in at six-thirty for their coffee. I'd never risen in time to see the lounge decked out in melons and croissants this way, appetizing and light. Everything remained at its permanent new tilt, and though the angle was slight it felt disconcerting to walk through the corridors, like walking down a stopped escalator: a swallowed lurch, an off-balance corner. The sun came out. People climbed outside and read on the tilted deck. Word came that the Coast Guard vessel the *Henry Larsen* would soon be on its way to rescue us. People assumed a festive air: one passenger began giving yoga lessons on the deck, and Aaju began a workshop at one of the café tables outside, showing people how to cut and sew seal skin.

I finally tucked my life jacket back in its emergency alcove. I'd hung over the side of the ship looking at the rock on which we were lodged, and had to admit we seemed pretty stable.

"Our location," came the briefing of our expedition leader over the loudspeakers, "is 67 degrees and 58 minutes north, and 112 degrees and 40 minutes west... near Home Islands...

the Duke of York Archipelago . . ." The loudspeaker crackled, obscuring the colonial name of another set of islands. "The list of the vessel remains constant. Our ballast tanks have leakage, but they are sacrificial. We know there is some damage to the hull. The stern is in three to four metres of water. The captain is trying to use the tides to alter the balance of the ship so it slides backward off the rock, but there are only thirty to forty centimetres between low and high tides."

Patience, the captain had told me, and I saw it now, as he joined me, looking down over the side of the ship at the rock from which he so badly wanted to deliver us. "Under our own steam," someone said, and I realized he did not want — no captain wants — his vessel or his passengers to have to be rescued by the coast guard. We watched, with the gradual change in tide, as the ship unloaded a couple of ten-ton lifeboats, reversed its engines, and activated the bow thrusters, pummelling water and creating a cantilever effect with the anchor in an effort to dislodge itself. But it stayed stuck fast.

Patience.

I saw the captain try again and again to free us, his face red with the effort of waiting for the tide to come a second time. Hours passed and passengers formed a book club, got out watercolours, planned a variety show. I discovered finally, after nearly two weeks on board the ship, where everyone else had been while I walked alone on the middle deck: they had been on the very top deck, a festive area covered in chaise longues and visited by kittiwakes, fulmars, and phalaropes, with endless sky above one's head: a birdwatcher's paradise. After everyone departed that deck at nightfall on our second stranded night, I stayed, and the northern lights visited as they had not done before on our journey, dancing and undulating green, mauve, and silver. I began dancing beneath them, keeping time with the lights by the tapping of my derelict hiking boots. I kept on late into the hours until a polite and diffident crew member came up the stairs, his buttons glittering in the aurora, and quietly admonished, "Please, Ma'am — the captain has asked if you would kindly not dance on his bedroom ceiling."

chapter nineteen

KUGLUKTUK

THE NEXT DAY the captain attempted again to propel the ship off the rock using engine power with the tides—the ship shuddered and made loud noises.

"The captain," our next briefing told us, "wouldn't try to move the ship if he thought it could cause more damage. He has talked to consulting captains offshore and they agree. However, there are variables and unknowns, and he will not take any action lightly or without all precautions."

I couldn't help but imagine what might happen if the ship did come free of the rock and be unable to float. How much damage had been done to the hull? What might happen if— then I saw Marc St-Onge. If there was anyone on board who might know what that rock was capable or not capable of doing to our ship . . .

"Hi, Marc."

"Hello, Kathleen."

"What, um . . ."

Marc must have known I was the world's worst geology student. My queries about rocks were like those I used to ask my science fiction professor in university: the questions of One Who Will Never Really Understand. Yet unlike my sci-fi prof, Marc was generous and forgiving, perhaps accustomed to my kind of obtuseness. Marc suffered fools gladly.

"What kind of rock would you say . . . I mean, do you know anything about what kind of rock it might be on which we've come aground?" I prepared to hear meticulous thought, hypotheses, open-ended insight.

"It's a gabbro sill. A horizontal but tilted—because everything is tilted—version of the columnar joints. I think this one will be well charted after this little incident."

According to our expedition leader, the rock had not been on the captain's charts: the soundings of Coronation Gulf we'd been following were labelled "various," which meant Franklin himself could have recorded some of them, and others may have been made at any time between Franklin's day and recent times.

The coast guard's *Henry Larsen* would not be rescuing us today as had been posited earlier. Instead, another vessel, the *Amundsen*, was on its way from where it had, with a crew of geologists, been mapping the ground beneath Arctic waters for a consortium of operators that included British Petroleum. It had been fitted out with twelve laboratories and considerable research equipment, so it was no longer merely an icebreaker. The *Amundsen*'s summer was taken up with mapping up-to-date soundings whose prior existence might, according to our ship's crew, have prevented our accident. Now the *Amundsen* was coming to rescue us at a maximum speed of sixteen and a half knots with hundreds of miles to travel. We would teeter on our gabbro sill for days. Anyone waiting for us at home would see our estimated time of arrival pass by without us.

In the library, our crew rigged up a couple of phones. It was hard to get a signal from our location to any town, and we were asked to keep our calls to a minute each. It would help, they said, if we talked and our families listened. I decided to call my husband's brother, as he sold houses so was glued to his cell phone, whereas my husband let his battery die or left the phone in his van while he climbed chimneys or leaned over the fence to hear Greek tomato cultivation lessons or talked to the beekeeper's wife about her new baby goat.

"Louis!" I yelled. Coronation Gulf to Montreal is around three and a half thousand kilometres.

"Kathleen? Aren't you supposed to be up North 'til tomorrow?"

"I've got one minute. Don't talk. I'm gonna do the talkin'."

"Okay!" Louis is a Dandenault, and Dandenaults catch on right away.

"We're okay. We're grounded on a rock. We're safe. But I'm not going to be home on time. We're going to be a few days late. Tell Jean. Tell him not to worry. But tell him not to go to the airport until he hears from me again."

"Are you sinking?" Dandenaults also know how to get the pertinent question out there.

"No. Bye."

"Okay. Bye."

Fifty-nine seconds — a perfect Winter-Dandenault transmission. Louis had the facts and I'd kept to my time limit and no one would panic at home. Back on deck I lay on my belly to read a book I'd found in the ship's library: *The Last Imaginary Place: A Human History of the Arctic World*, by Robert McGhee.

"A trail of skeletons, equipment and personal belongings led southward to the Arctic coast," McGhee wrote of the Franklin remnants, "where all traces of the expedition vanished . . ." While searchers never found the ships, he went on, "they did accomplish another goal: that of mapping the interconnected channels that comprise the Northwest Passage . . ."

Our deck at its new and stationary angle felt warm, the ship no longer shuddering with the tides, as we resigned ourselves to await rescue. McGhee, who'd written the book three years before, described the nineteenth-century idea of an Arctic possessing "crystalline fortresses looming under skies that glow with fantastic auroras or blaze with multiple suns linked by arches and rings of light... the sense of an other-world . . ."

It was strange, shipwrecked a day's sail shy of our intended goal of Kugluktuk, to be reading McGhee's book. Strange, because all that he outlined still existed: we'd been part of it, on our voyage. We'd traced Franklin's route, we'd seen the crystalline fortresses and fantastic auroras, and we'd found, within this world, an other-world of extraordinary physical and psychological properties I'd previously encountered only as a hint, a glimmering thread. Now we balanced motionless in that world, waiting for a ship called the *Amundsen* — after the man who'd been first to traverse those interconnected channels of which McGhee wrote. But before it was named the

Amundsen, the ship now on its way to rescue us had possessed another name: in 1979, when it was built in North Vancouver, it had been christened the CCGS *Sir John Franklin*.

We did the very things I'd read lost Arctic expeditions do while hoping someone will come to their rescue. We had our variety show—my favourite piece was the choir Yoko orchestrated among her Japanese travellers, including the beautiful Motoko with her leg still in a cast. Ken McGoogan sang Bill Staines's song "The Roseville Fair," and I hauled out my concertina and sang a penny broadsheet ballad Johnny Burke used to sing in St. John's at the turn of the century. A call came on the loudspeaker urgently requesting duct tape to pack boxes of books to be evacuated from the ship's library, and I triumphantly produced the roll my daughter had advised me to bring.

For two nights and the better part of three days we waited, until, that third day, word came that the *Amundsen* would be alongside our vessel by nightfall. It would send small covered boats to the hanging staircase we'd descended so many times to hike on the land, and we would take the arms of Coast Guard staff and let them usher us onto their vessel. We were to wait until our names were called.

Since my surname starts with W, I was used to being among the last to be called wherever I went. Now, this felt like a reprieve: I could walk around our ship one last time and say goodbye to it. On deck I had the impulse to remove my decrepit boots and leave them suspended in the North: I tied them, their tongues lolling against ripped leather mouths, to a lifebuoy lashed onto the railings. Someone would find them, I knew, as our captain and crew would not be abandoning ship with us. They had to stay on board until towing outfits came to free the vessel or it recovered — increasingly unlikely — to sail on its own steam, back to dry dock for repairs. So I lashed the boots, readied my bags, and sat to wait for my name, when Nathan showed up with his guitar, wanting to sing me one last song. He didn't have to ask which one. He knew it would have to be Archie Fisher's "Dark Eyed Molly," which Ken McGoogan and I had agreed we could listen to Nathan sing over and over until the world ended. I sat and listened to Nathan's caramel-and-tar voice begin that song again, my heart full of all that had happened on this journey.

He was halfway through the song when over the loud-speaker, far from its place in the alphabet, blared my name. I didn't want to hear it. I did not want to leave the song.

"I'll sing the rest for you sometime on land," Nathan said, and I turned my back on him and headed for the door gaping onto the gulf. I saw the coast guard boats with their orange tarps — cellophane windows lining the decks — chugging our people to the big red *Amundsen*. It struck me that the coast guard rescuers, decked out in overalls, reflector strips, and canary yellow hard hats, altered the collective and individual identities of our passengers, who'd been intrepid adventurers all this time. Now the coast guard took each of us by the arm as if we were little old ladies and frail old men, traumatized and in shock. The coast guard, big and young, strong and benevolent, had come to extricate us from... well, from peril and danger and fright. They seemed to neither realize nor care that we'd spent the last three days, not tearfully scanning the horizon with scopes for signs of our salvation, but lolling on our tilted deck discussing Arctic philosophy, winding our knees behind our necks in yoga poses, and making merry in the lounge with renditions of apple-blossom haiku and Scottish ballads. They seemed to have no idea we'd been happy, even euphoric—except for our almost-forgotten hour of dread—or that we were reluctant to leave our beloved vessel. They extended rubberized and paternalistic arms, cradling our frail forms, ushering us into the tarpaulined dinghies, then tearing through the splashing foam—some of us sang and I heard harmonicas playing—toward the great and looming *Amundsen*.

It was hard, given the cloudy plastic windows, to see the vessel we were leaving behind, her captain and crew still aboard. I craned and ignored admonishments to hunker down—I wanted one last good look at our beloved ship, and I got it. I saw the injury done to her by that gabbro sill, her nose jutting out of the water and the dark red hull, normally submerged, now rising in the air—our ship, her graceful blue and white lines, her flags, her portholes—indisputably marooned.

At that time many of us believed our vessel might, with help, be able to sail to port once freed from the rock. But in fact our grounding had been severe, and it would take nearly three weeks and many trials to free the ship. According to a subsequent marine investigation report, gusting winds and high seas in the first week of September made the stranded ship roll, pitch, and pound the sea floor, complicating the damage already done to its hull and diesel tanks. It would take a dive team and many salvage attempts to finally free her and get her to Cambridge Bay, and subsequently to Greenland, Iceland,

and Gdańsk to complete the necessary repairs.

But on the *Amundsen* we did not realize any of this. We did think about the crew, and I wondered what they would eat and how long they'd have to wait there. But our collective view of our abandoned ship — our memory of it — was still that of a magical vessel, where we'd known beauty and the great thrill of the North.

We reached Kugluktuk at sunrise. In open dinghies someone said were properly called Hurricanes, the coast guard transferred us to the shore that had been the destination of eighteenth-century explorer Samuel Hearne: the area known to Inuit as Kugluktuk but colonially named Coppermine. In many respects the map Hearne used wasn't all that different from the ones we'd been consulting 230 years after him. Debates raged as to the accuracy of this and that mark or sounding, and questions would arise, in the months following our voyage, as to why our charts had not prepared us for the rock that grounded our vessel. Had our charts been up to date or had they not? In media stories written in both New and Old worlds about our Arctic accident, few failed to mention that there were yet-unmapped parts of the Arctic waters. As told to me by another of the geologists, Steve, on the *Amundsen*, the process of mapping the North was going on even as we spoke. "You," Steve said, gesturing to Nathan, Sheena, Ken, and all who'd shared our route's history and archeology, geography and song, "are part of the charting."

The people of Kugluktuk lent us their recreation complex.

We chose spots on the floor upon which to cover ourselves in coats and roll sweaters for pillows to get an hour of sleep. Villagers sent us packets of fruit juice and snacks meant for their children's school lunches. I bunked down beside a soccer goal-post but didn't get much sleep. I went out and met children playing with a husky pup, and when they put the pup in my arms I felt that unconditional connection I always feel with a dog—suddenly, things seemed not quite so forlorn, despite the overtiredness that had overtaken all but Motoko, whom I'd seen applying lipstick before a hand-held mirror as she sat on the floor, her cast propped in front of her.

A Canadian North aircraft landed to take us back to the south. I stood in a lineup with Elisabeth and Nathan as we awaited a processing procedure clearly not meant for our volume of people or baggage. Nathan showed Elisabeth some martial art balancing exercises and she mimicked a blue heron standing on one leg, her hands and her free leg ambulating high, serene and triumphant. I tried balancing on one leg but wobbled like a drunken punching clown while they moved on to a graceful exhibition of swordsmanship without swords. I seemed to be the only person trying to conceal tears behind toy sunglasses.

On the plane I found myself next to a quiet woman I'd not gotten to know on the voyage. She was small, long-haired, and travelling, it appeared, alone. I felt the aircraft lift away from the sacred land, into air that would take me back to ordinary life, and were it not for the strangeness of what my seatmate said I might have let it slip, unheard, past my tears.

"Are they women or birds?" She pointed out the window

at the wing — somehow nearly every flight I've taken puts me just behind the wing. I saw blue sky, no clouds.

"Birds? I guess we've passed them."

"No. There — look."

"I see no birds."

"Maybe they're women."

How could there be women outside our plane, in the sky? I looked at my companion more carefully, then followed the line along which she pointed. I saw indentations on the wing, darker than other parts. I don't know anything about aircraft design, but . . . could she think these features on the wing were women or birds?

"Do you mean —" I pointed to the dark areas.

"Yes! You do see them. Are they women? Or birds?"

I realized this woman was in another world, and throughout the preceding days, in Greenland and crossing the tundra and all the while we'd traversed the route of Franklin and found cairns and bones and kettles of lost expeditions, snow geese and polar bears and red-throated loons, someone, or several someones — angels on the voyage with us — must have been looking after this woman, keeping her safe, caring and making sure she didn't become more lost or confused than she already was. It was my turn now and I gently told her the four bird women were part of the aircraft, made of shadows and sections of wing. I agreed it was a trick of the light and, yes, shadows could appear to be what they were not. We continued like this all the way to Edmonton, and by the time we began our descent into the airport my face had dried.

chapter twenty

SACRED LAND

My TIME IN the North had given me a new sense, like sight, or touch—like hearing, but the receptive organ was my whole self, a self that no longer felt separate from the land.

After I got home, I couldn't stop thinking about both the North itself, alive *now* at the top of the world, and the history of the North as told by people who held wildly different points of view. I knew that in New York City sat one particular piece of Northern history that contained aspects of all these stories: it was a living piece of the land, yet emanated stories both Inuit and European. It also spoke from a place, far more distant, that looked down on all our human stories from a whole other perspective. This piece of North that I wanted to see and touch was the meteorite Robert Peary had transported, in 1897, from Savissivik, Greenland, where it had lain for millennia: celestial iron from which generations of Greenlandic people had hammered pieces to form their hunting tools—until Peary took it away.

"I never thought I'd see the day," I told friends, "I'd go out of my way to look at a giant rock, but that's what going North did to me. That's what being on a ship with a rock evangelist, and getting grounded on a piece of gabbro sill, has done to me."

Peary had to build a section of railway — the only railroad in Greenland — in order to roll that iron out of its realm and get it aboard the *Hope*, a 370-ton steamer he'd brought along for the job. It took him five years. There were actually three pieces of meteorite; hunters told Peary they had named them Ahnighito (the Tent), the Woman, and the Dog. They told him a story about these three forms, then he took all three away and gave them to his wife, who sold them to the American Museum of Natural History for $40,000.

I told Bernadette Dean I intended to go and see Ahnighito.

"You will have to read," she said, "how they had to tear down walls and such to get that meteor into the Museum of Natural History."

"They did?"

"Yes, and while you're at it, there's something else at that museum. My great-grandmother's tuilli is there too, but in storage."

I remembered Bernadette telling me the story of Shoofly, the woman who fell in love with a Boston whaling captain and gave him beadwork and handmade garments, which Bernadette had a hard time getting the folks at the museum to agree to show her. I'd thought a lot about that scene, Bernadette feeling like she'd felt at Sir John Franklin High School — an Inuit kid being told by white teachers about their version of her world and everything in it. I'd researched and sketched pictures of what the garments might have looked like. Now I became excited.

"Do you think," I asked her, "there's any way they will let me see Shoofly's tuilli?"

"Ask to see Laila Williamson and tell her you know me — you might have to call her in advance — and they can bring you to the storage room where it is, as well as her leggings — stockings — and hair ornaments."

I left a phone message for Laila Williamson. She returned it that afternoon.

"Pictures of Shoofly's clothing," she told me, "are on the internet. Why don't you just look at them online? The photographs were professionally done and you'll be able to see all the details."

"I'm coming to the museum anyway, to see Ahnighito and the Woman and the Dog . . ." As I said the names aloud I began to feel they were personal acquaintances, living beings and not insensate at all. "I'll be in New York all weekend."

"Ah, well then, it will be impossible for you to see the garments because we are not open to the public during the weekend — only on weekdays."

"I understand, but I haven't bought my return ticket yet — just a one-way bus fare. I haven't decided whether to come back by bus or train, so I could come back home any day."

It seemed a shame, Laila hinted, to hang around unnecessarily when I could go home on Sunday as originally planned, especially since the garments were so well represented online.

"Sometimes," I said carefully, gently, not wanting to seem

obnoxious or argumentative, "seeing a thing, being in the same room with it, being *in its presence*, well, I'm a writer, and I...things can speak to me differently when I'm with them in the room . . ."

I fell silent.

"All right, then. You'll have to fill out a visitor research form."

I took my daughter Esther to New York with me. We'd had a riot together when we travelled to London a few years earlier, climbing up St. Paul's and careering around on the top tier of a double-decker bus eye-level with brooding statuary that had threatened to come alive and drag us to Arthurian forests. At Stonehenge we ate cheese and onion sandwiches with our backs to the stones as Virginia Woolf had done, and somehow we couldn't stop laughing at Englishness and how little it ever changed.

But New York was different. When our bus let us off at 4:30 in the morning at 8th Avenue and 42nd Street, I was terrified to leave the station.

"Come on, Mom," Esther said. "They're just New Yorkers, they're just people living." She dragged me in and out of the Lucky Star Café. We passed Tiffany's, costumes from the Brooklyn Museum, and window displays of the newest shirts covered in feathers and hair. Men in shirts labelled NYC *Street to Home Outreach* bent over a woman whose sign read, *Leave me alone — I want nothing.* Rockefeller Centre's rink was tiny — but then so was Stonehenge — gold silk flags, giant trees, guards. Beautiful, quiet Bryant Park rested, birds asleep in the trees, then the stone library lions. In London we'd yelled,

"Stop it!" to Buckingham Palace and all the statues, but New York made us exclaim, "Bring it on!" with its exuberant, joyful possibility.

On Monday, Esther went home and I headed for the Museum of Natural History's 77th Street entrance. The museum tower rose, imposing, over Central Park and into the sky. Laila Williamson, accompanied by a museum guard, came to meet me. Laila was a kind of woman I enjoy: severe, unadorned and unsmiling, a woman who walks everywhere. The guard melted away and Laila whisked me into darkness, past — it had to be — looming, glittering, *massive*. . .

"Is that—"

"The Cape York meteorite, Anhighito, yes."

We zoomed past Ahnighito and Laila swung open opaque glass doors bearing prohibitive signs. We ascended an elevator closed to the public, then, corridors . . . wall space covered in tall cabinets that I surmised must contain items acquired by the museum but not displayed in its galleries. We passed workers at desks and entered a back room painted grey, with more closed cabinets, and on a table laid out in clinical fashion on a length of paper lay Shoofly's garment, the tuilli of Bernadette's great-grandmother who fell in love with and was made love to and photographed and yearned for and returned to by whaling captain George Comer with whom she sailed on ocean journeys and bore, it was said, a son everyone called John.

"The garment's accession number," Laila said, "is 1902: the year George Comer brought it in. You can see it's worn. She used to walk around in it — it shows the regular dirt of wearing." She fingered a piece of the fine-cut fringe that had loosened. "Caribou sheds terribly. There's a photo of her sewing with a sewing machine, but I think this is all hand sewn. It's hard to sew hide with a machine."

Laila had me sign a visiting researcher imaging agreement, promising I'd seek permission to publish any photographs I took, though there were photographs online of Shoofly wearing the garment — anyone could look at it without resorting to photographs of mine. I was struck by how flat the tuilli was laid out. It reminded me of salt fish on wooden flakes, not on Newfoundland beaches but in museums that claimed to portray Newfoundland as it was before the death of the cod fishery. I bent closer and saw that Bernadette's great-grandmother had sewn living scenes on the breastplate.

"Comer's ships," Laila said, "stayed over the winter. He lived partly with the Eskimos at the time. She was from the Aivilik group."

Eskimos. I had not heard anyone say that word in a long time — did they still say it in America? I tried to imagine how I might feel if someone called my grandmother or great-grandmother "a Northumbrian brick-maker descended from examples of the Pictish-Gael merger," while guarding one of her crocheted blankets for the archives. But I couldn't imagine it, and even had I been able, it wouldn't have been the same.

I felt death around the tuilli all laid out and flattened. I felt it in the labels *Eskimo* and *Aivilik*, in the tower on this building, and in the whole edifice with its topiary and tiny windows and its titles chiselled in the lintels. This was a tomb. Anyone alive in here was involved in classification of things murdered, like the thousands of living, winged miracles caught by Audubon and by the butterfly collectors and all colonial explorers from the European Age of Sail until now.

"This—" I gestured to one of Shoofly's beaded scenes on the hood of the tuilli, a story that must have taken as long to make as it took any scientist or documentary filmmaker or writer to create a scene of daily life anywhere.

"It's a hunting scene," said Laila Williamson. "Hunting caribou."

The beads were red, yellow, black, blue, and white, except for the hunter, in green pants and a pink shirt. The caribou was red and over the scene hung resplendent stars.

Bernadette had told me she'd written a piece about the tuilli for an exhibit called *Infinity of Nations* at the National Museum of the American Indian. In it she called the caribou-hunting scene her favourite image on the garment. She told me Shoofly would have loved knowing her descendants still hunt caribou and harvest skins for clothing and boots. In the piece, she said her elders told her parts of the designs were suggested to Shoofly by George Comer, and she wondered if those might be the stars or the breastplate's geometric forms. But those forms, I saw, looked like the pods, flowers, and seeds I'd seen in the Arctic. And what was this, also on the breastplate— a pair of Victorian walking boots? They had sturdy but fashionable heels and looked to me like old-fashioned European boots with hooks and buttons, definitely not for walking over the tundra.

Bernadette would tell me, when I later asked her about the boots, that George Comer gave Shoofly a pair of dainty European boots for walking the sidewalks of London or New York with an umbrella in your hand as you fed pigeons or ogled, as my daughter and I had done, spangles hung round a black velvet throat inside Tiffany's plate glass. Comer gave Shoofly boots to which any woman might thrill, be she in brogues like Laila Williamson's or in the decrepit specimens I'd lashed to our abandoned Arctic ship. Comer gave Shoofly boots a lover gives a woman, but he had another life with another wife so did not every night caress Shoofly's feet with his hands. Or maybe he was simply not the most observant man or maybe he stole the boots of Julia, his white wife, for Shoofly, thinking all women's feet were the same. In any event, the boots were too small, and what did Shoofly do with a pair of mouth-watering boots that didn't fit? She sewed their image on her tuilli in beads so she could walk the land displaying their glory anyway.

"Are you working on anything exciting now?" I asked Laila Williamson. I sensed she wished to get back to other preoccupations.

"As a matter of fact, we've just received a collection from Indians of western Mexico . . ."

Downstairs, Ahnighito waited for me. Beside it, much smaller, stood the Woman and the Dog. I felt as I had when I sat on ground in the North with rocks that stood under the Arctic sky. For once, the flight impulse of a mind inclined to immaterial things had come home, was tethered and nourished by the ground. Ground is both magnet and celestial body, hurtling in space and attracting other bodies. Ahnighito, the Woman, and the Dog are like my husband's giant hand on my heart when I'm nervous or sad. They have a wordless power, a comfort, and they speak using not words but substance — the inchoate origin of all words. The Dog is little and smooth — like a real dog, in proportion to Ahnighito and the Woman — a playful and beloved one. I could see how Greenlandic people had chipped pieces for their tools, leaving pockmarks, organic and purposeful, before being interrupted by Peary, who won their confidence then made the Dog, Tent, and Woman disappear.

"*Spectacular samples from around the planet...*" booms a generic film voiceover from the display room next door. A woman and her children traipse past Ahnighito, and the mother gives a textbook explanation of meteorites without glancing at Ahnighito, the Dog, or the Woman.

We were using it, I imagine I hear a hunter tell Peary.

Upstairs I knew Laila Williamson might be carefully folding Shoofly's tuilli away. I had not asked her if I could also see Shoofly's leggings and hair ornaments. Laila Williamson had been courteous and forthcoming, yet I felt sad somehow. Sitting with Ahnighito and its companions, touching them, feeling where hunters once scooped metal from the Woman and the heartbreaking, curved Dog — why couldn't Peary have left the Greenlandic people the Dog, the Woman, and their shelter, Ahnighito?

I later asked Bernadette where Ahnighito's name came from.

"We have a word in our language, in my dialect — *angijuq* — for large, or big. So the word you wrote down has the same roots, but men — English-speaking men — at that time wrote differently or guessed at the word."

The Museum of Natural History makes allowances for guesswork while remaining as precise and scientific as it can. "Medium octahedrite," it calls the specific iron composition of Ahnighito, while proclaiming on a plaque that the story of the Tent, the Woman, and the Dog might have been made up by hunters especially for Peary, to please him. The stone sits unknown and unheard by the hordes that do what people do in museums—they come to learn, but what are they learning?

LATER, ON A January day in Montreal, the sun shone and I was aware that the tundra was not under my feet. Rue Jean-Talon was under my feet, its sidewalks covered in ice. Grace notes that morning were limited to a flight of pigeons from drugstore eave to dilapidated bus shelter. I walked past an apartment block and noticed for a second time that week that while it was minus sixteen degrees Celsius, a grate emitted gusts of air warm as a summer day. Our prime minister had told world leaders at the latest European summit on the global economy that there was no point in setting caps on greenhouse gas emissions because to do so was unrealistic. The Spanish prime minister looked at him as if he were from another planet, and responded that if we did not change our behaviour globally, we'd perish.

Montreal's trees were not in their glory. They had no leaves. Starlings and pigeons chose to roost in gutters and on sills instead, leaving the trees bare, bark cracked and gleaming with ice under a frozen sky. Passersby ignored the trees: dog walkers, office workers hurrying with coffee in paper cups, old women huffing with canes and bags of apples and toilet paper.

I remembered how, years ago, I'd sensed a glory within such ordinary things: starlings, branches, the humble loveliness of alleys or weeds in vacant lots. Yet I'd felt, even when young, that along with its loveliness the earth faced an elusive threat about which no one spoke: we went on as if life as we knew it, in our fortunate part of the world, would chug on forever.

Even now, people continued to act this way, when everyone had heard at least some alarm bells clanging about dangers to the planet. It astonished me that we remained so capable of "business as usual" when the rules of life had so obviously altered.

Though bare and cracked, the winter city trees had a vocabulary of bud and intersecting branches reaching up, interlaced and poignant in their yearning for light: they had *presence*, and it was a presence I now felt if I concentrated on listening, on intercepting in the way the Arctic land had taught me. A tree had a body as I have a body. Its roots reached deep for clear water. We forgot about the roots and how powerful trees were; not powerful in self-defence or advancement, or in any of the frontier-busting, action-packed kinds of power commonly understood, but powerful in presence and gravity. If I listened and received what the trees had to say, even winter city trees, I heard the story of someone beautiful going unheard. What did the earth say as we hurried on our quotidian errands? It said, *"Listen! Something new is going on."*

Since coming back south I had not been the same. Every leaf, rock, and cloud now spoke to me of the North, and the message the North had been trying to tell me. I looked around to see who — if anyone — might be hearing and acting on that message. At night on the news I learned the Canadian government had sent out a press release: it had tallied the amount of money a polar bear might be worth if you counted meat, fur, tourism, and other ways the animal might contribute to the Gross National Product. Peter Mansbridge announced this with his usual anchorman's combination of gravitas and bonhomie, the tone implying *here we have a sound idea,* but what I saw was a tabulation of monetary value without care for any of the deeper meaning of a bear, or land, or people in the North: I sensed the old colonial method of calculating value. But at the same time a new concept — a word — reached me through my daughter Juliette, studying climate and geography in high school.

The word was "cryosphere," one of those rare scientific words that manage to hold a profoundly human and sacred resonance. From the Greek *cryos,* meaning cold, frost, or ice, and *sphaira,* meaning globe or ball, the word refers to that part of planet Earth that remains frozen: a part we now know to be melting and shrinking while we cling to global political, cultural, and industrial policies that accelerate the melt. The word cryosphere was a new utterance, one not in my Oxford dictionary, and in my mind the word itself drifted apart, like pieces of melting ice, into the utterance, "Cry, O Sphere." It became part of a lament that lived in me as I wondered how I should live, now that I had returned south.

Cry, O sphere — weep, dear globe; lament, people, if ground this sacred should go unheard . . . Cry, O sphere, if I should walk

in the North and perceive only earth's mineral body and not her
sacred mind . . .

I missed Bernadette Dean and Aaju Peter — their voices
and their points of view. But another aboriginal woman was
making her voice heard. Chief Theresa Spence of Canada's
Attawapiskat reserve had begun a hunger strike to protest her
people's living conditions. Meanwhile, First Nations people
across Canada had begun opposing new federal legislation that
stripped protection from rivers, lakes, and land for economic
gain. Indigenous groups and their allies from New Zealand,
South America, Africa, the U.S., and Israel had joined Canada's First Nations in proclaiming the end of a global adher-
ence to old, colonial models that treated life as a commodity
rather than a sacred trust. I decided to go by bus to visit Chief
Spence's teepee on the site of her protest, a tiny island in the
Ottawa River.

I arrived in Ottawa on day 31 of Chief Spence's fast. Taxi
drivers and shopkeepers just a fifteen-minute walk away from
the protest site had no idea what was going on there. When
I asked for directions to Chief Spence's teepee, or mentioned
her hunger strike, people did not know where it was or what
it was about. My husband had warned me, back in Montreal,
that what looked to me like the start of a global uprising was
going unnoticed by most people, rushing as usual to get to
work on time.

I walked in the snow past the Château Laurier toward the
island marked on my map as Victoria Island. Soon I was on
Wellington Street, walking directly in front of the Parliament Buildings. It was not long after Christmas and dusk had

fallen. Giant snowflakes of red, green, and white light were projected onto the austere stone of the buildings; the Centennial Flame undulated in its font as tourists hung around taking photos. I knew Victoria Island should be behind Parliament Hill, but I couldn't see it. The Peace Tower and Centre Block rose up with a face and shoulders that felt imposing and damning at the same time. Who did I think I was, walking past these halls of power in old rubber boots with three hard-boiled eggs, a twist of salt in tinfoil, and a Thermos of Labrador tea in my backpack?

I dreaded finding myself on some cloverleaf autoroute not meant for human walking. I feared getting lost and never finding Theresa Spence or her teepee. I'd travelled here alone, a ragamuffin interloper who had no right walking past the Flame or the Queen's Gates with sympathies on which the lofty clock face might well look down with suspicion. Did Wellington Street never end? But there, to the right, I saw the Portage Bridge, its divided lanes full of traffic whizzing past and darkness on either side. I'd envisioned it as a smaller bridge from which I could look down and see Victoria Island, and travel perhaps down some stairs and see the teepee plainly from the road. But all I saw was blackness. Why had I even come?

It would have been easy to rationalize going home, and some would have supposed I'd finally seen sense. But I kept walking. On which side of the bridge was her teepee? What right had I to approach the chief's encampment? I kept walking and I listened to the consciousness that I had learned, in the Arctic, to discern in the land, water and air. While the bridge remained covered in traffic, I sensed the water of the

Ottawa River beneath it, and I could see blackness where the trees grew thickly. The moon, which had been full the night before, illuminated the sky above the Parliament Buildings that now towered behind me. As I asked the land for guidance, I began to tune out the cars and to watch the snow at the edge of the bridge. I neared its end now: what if I reached it without finding an opening?

Then, lit gold and blue in the darkened snow, I noticed a trail of footprints leading off the bridge, to my right and down the embankment. I followed them until I saw sticks pointing above a fence: the star-shaped apex of the teepee, inside an enclosure of rough wood. There was no sound, though I saw smoke rising from inside, and there was a gate through which I saw the flickering of a fire. The gate was ajar. A young man guarded it and I sensed I needed to speak my purpose.

What *was* my purpose, exactly? Why was this place so quiet? Two women played with a child around the fire. The child had a drum. I saw trees, and a shack, and the smoke of another fire from behind a lean-to.

"Hi," I said to the young man.

"Hi."

I liked the way nothing about him challenged my right to be there, yet he somehow invited me to speak my thoughts.

"I came on the bus from Montreal. I hope it's okay. I wanted to pay my respects to Chief Spence . . . her hunger strike. Is it okay if I come in and do that?"

"Sure. She's sleeping now. But you can come in. You can make an offering of tobacco if you want."

I thanked him and went in as if I knew what he was talking

about. An offering of tobacco? I didn't know what that meant, and I certainly had no tobacco on me. It struck me as kind of him to assume I had an offering of any kind. I had brought a small gift for the chief, but it was not tobacco.

The child with the drum chanted and drummed in a voice more powerful and prophetic than I could have imagined. The second fire, glowing behind the lean-to, was the sacred fire of Chief Spence and her supporters: there were traditions that had to be kept around the fire, one of them being that I must not take out my notebook or record anything on camera. The woman I call my sister outlaw, Christine — the one who had given me the Viking funeral to cleanse me of the old ghosts from my first marriage — had come from Toronto, and on that first night I found her sitting with the four or five others who were praying and conversing around the flames. We'd thought the island would be so full of people we might not be able to fit. But here we were, with fewer than a dozen others: an elder who alternated between prayers and jokes, the drumming boy and his mother, and a woman who told me about hiding out in the desert around the Canada-U.S. border, managing to feed her children while evading border guards for years.

I took in the fragrance of smudged sage and the comfort of the flames in near-solitude, and much quietness. This sacred fire gave me old blessings I knew I had been missing.

I walked to the tree down by the river, where people had tied bright prayer ties with tobacco inside them, and I looked across the river at how close the Parliament Buildings towered. This little island was tucked right in the centre of Canadian history like a stone in the setting of a ring. I wondered what its name had been before it was named after Victoria, and I remembered all the Arctic landmarks that possessed two names: a British colonial appellation superimposed over the name given by the original peoples.

That night, by the fire, the child with the drum sang:

I remember the time
When we used to stay up all night, singing
Aiee hai away . . . Aiee hai awa . . .

IN THE MORNING I heard, from across the river, the rumbling hum of the machinery that kept the city running. Here on the island were sounds of chopping wood, honking Canada geese, a squeaking gate, snow creaking underfoot, then drums and singing in the chief's teepee as healers attended her. Elders had begun to gather and I overheard them ask each other, "How are we nourishing the next generation of future elders, the people who are forty and fifty years old now?"

I'd begun to hear whispers that the new movement to protect the earth was a movement led by women. More people gathered, and I learned news media would be descending that afternoon; members of Parliament were coming, and the chief had a message she wanted to speak to the world.

I had my small gift for the chief and I wanted to give it to someone before the crowds arrived, so I asked a large, friendly man in a fur hat outside her teepee if there was a place I could leave it.

"It's Labrador tea I picked in Newfoundland."

I also had a card depicting a muskox in the snow, tiny in the photograph. It was a lonely animal, I felt, after having seen how Arctic muskoxen in Dundas Harbour had huddled to form one warm mountain. The chief must, herself, feel alone now in spite of the gathering crowd. No one else had yet joined her in fasting.

The man's face lit up. "Thank you. I'll give it to her."

He took the bag of pungent leaves as if it were frankincense or myrrh. I'd worried it might feel silly to give such a small thing, but he made me feel I'd given something of myself, of my time, and of the land, and I had. I'd spent a whole sunlit afternoon on a height of land on the west coast of Newfoundland, picking the tea and remembering other tea harvests I'd made with my old friend Art Andrews on the Witless Bay Barrens. The tea was fragrant with medicine, filled with Newfoundland sun, and full of personal memories — I'd picked it to use myself, but at the last minute, before leaving Montreal, it had occurred to me to bring it to the chief, who was drinking medicinal tea while she fasted. If I had not known enough to bring tobacco, I thought now, at least this kind man accepted what I had thought to bring.

As the journalists gathered I noticed one young writer without a camera. Clad in a fedora and scribbling on the kind of steno notebook I'd been trained to use in journalism school, he weighed hardly more than a hundred pounds. His goatee had caught snowflakes that had melted then re-crystallized, and his tone gave him an air of hysteria as he interrogated the man who'd taken my Labrador tea. This gatekeeper, I noticed, was much more patient than I am when people talk to me aggressively.

"Who are you, anyway?" asked the scribe. "A firekeeper?"

"No."

"Not a firekeeper? Then who?"

"A peacekeeper."

"Keeping the peace between who?"

"Between everyone."

I considered moving out of earshot but felt intrigued by the contrast between the shrill interrogator and his respondent. I found myself judging the writer, thinking myself more gentle than he was, though this was far from true, and I couldn't tear myself away, especially when he asked a question I had been wondering about.

"What is the previous name of this island?"

"This is Victoria Island."

"But what is the aboriginal name for it? What do you call it?"

"We call it Victoria Island."

The goateed man went into a diatribe about how it couldn't really be called Victoria Island. Wasn't it unceded Algonquin land? Wasn't "Victoria" a colonial appellation? Hadn't the peacekeeper enough sense to realize his people couldn't possibly have called this island Victoria Island in the beginning?

"We called it," came the reply in a quiet voice, "Island of the Pipe."

Goatee boy either did not hear or had built up such momentum in his rapid-fire questioning that he launched into a new topic. I lost the ability to keep my mouth shut.

"Excuse me," I said to the keeper of my gift, "*Island of the Pipe* — can you say any more about it?"

"Because of the rapids," he said, "the water narrows, and the power of it causes steam to rise up, like smoke from a pipe."

"It's sacred land though, right?" the goateed man challenged. I was not sure what he wanted. He appeared to have written nothing about the Island of the Pipe and now kept repeating his question about sacred land. "Is it sacred, this location? Is that why you've chosen it for the hunger strike?"

He continued asking whether the island was sacred, and again it appeared to me he did not hear the answer, spoken in so low a voice, ever so softly, but it entered my body quite powerfully so that I could not mistake it.

"All land is sacred," said the keeper of the peace.

ALL LAND IS SACRED. The place we call the Northwest Passage had taught me this was true, and all through the next spring and summer I saw that my voyage had attuned me to natural things no matter how insignificant: a piece of goldenrod growing in the crack between Carrefour Dental Clinic and Rue Belanger's sidewalk; squirrels in the Italian park on Boulevard St-Laurent; a tree full of tiny birds in a patch of sunlight on Mozart Street. I wanted more of this, so I bought a one-person tent and went out on the land.

I had met a medicine woman who'd taught me how to find a place to fast and live for several days, consulting wind, animals, trees, stones, and the cardinal directions. Even after my time in the North, I was unprepared for how instructive the land is if you give yourself to it, without distraction, and listen. I'd begun reading Evelyn Eaton's book *I Send a Voice*, and had come to the part where she warns how important it is to keep private all that the land and the animals will share with a person who is truly listening, lest people fail to understand, or mock.

"The omens, the intimations that come," writes Eaton, a Swiss-born Canadian poet, novelist, and lecturer who devoted her later years to the spirituality of her eastern-Canadian aboriginal roots, "the Presences who make themselves felt, the responses of the natural world, animals who come to be blessed...flowers opening wider, grasses leaning forward, water in the stream drumming with a new sound and rhythm, these things cannot be discussed without losing force, or being taken for coincidence, or even jeered at...But they can be discovered, felt and understood by those who will sit in commitment and integrity . . ."

I took my tent to a clearing in woods, surrounded by pines. I would spend days and nights alone, with no food, no book, and no companion save for those the land provided. In the night, deer came close—I heard their whooshing exclamations of breath as they neared my tent. Paying attention, for the first time in my life, to the four directions, I said goodbye to flock after flock of geese starting their journeys south, their streamlined calligraphy echoed in the V-shaped needle patterns in the pines. Nothing will happen, I thought at first, but I'd promised to wait.

Hours into my silence, the oldest pine shared a fragment of its silent knowledge. I began to experience the connection I'd begun to know in the Arctic, and what Evelyn Eaton called the responses of the natural world—subtle yet unmistakable—audible only if I agreed to remain with the land instead of insisting on passing through.

Eaton was right in saying these messages from the natural world need, for a time, at least, to remain secret. For the first time in my life, I'd begun to ask questions not of human teachers, but of a crow, a white stone, a deer in the night. I cannot say here all that the land began teaching me on that first consultation I undertook after returning from the North: much of it was meant for me to hear and act on alone, and is still only the whisper of a new voyage, just barely beginning.

ACKNOWLEDGEMENTS

THANK YOU, Bernadette Dean, Aaju Peter, Sheena Fraser McGoogan, Nathan Rogers, Elisabeth Richard-Moscovitz, and all my kind companions on the journey. Thank you to the teachers on board our vessel, especially Marc St-Onge for your patience and insight regarding the importance of rock. Thank you to Matthew Swan and Adventure Canada for your generous hospitality, and to Noah Richler for the invitation to embark. Thank you, Rebecca Burgum, for your gentle kindness. Thank you, Laila Williamson of the American Museum of Natural History, for showing and describing to me the garments of Shoofly. I thank everyone at House of Anansi, especially Sarah MacLachlan, my dedicated editor Janie Yoon, and the book's designer Alysia Shewchuk. Thank you, Melanie Little, for your elegant copy-editing. Thank you to my agent, Shaun Bradley, for your unfailing insight, support, and good judgment. Thank you Lois Carson, for reading and

commenting on the manuscript. Thank you, Christine Pount-
ney, for your sacred ministrations. Thank you to my family
and friends, and to the living land, without whom I would suffer great loneliness. And thank you, dear reader.

Lyrics from "The Turning" written by Nathan Rogers, copy-
right 2011 Dry Bones Music, Winnipeg, Canada, have been
gratefully reproduced with kind permission from the artist.

I am indebted to Elisabeth Richard-Moscovitz for sharing with
me her memories of our journey, which helped me remember
details I might have missed or forgotten.

The poem quoted in Chapter One is William Wordsworth's
"Ode on Intimations of Immortality from Recollections of
Early Childhood." All other quotations have their sources
indicated where they occur throughout the book.

KATHLEEN WINTER is the author of the bestselling novel
Annabel, which won the Thomas Raddall Atlantic Fiction
Award and was a finalist for the Scotiabank Giller Prize, the
Governor General's Literary Award, the Rogers Writers'
Trust Fiction Prize, the Orange Prize for Fiction, and CBC
Canada Reads. Her first collection of stories, *boYs*, won both
the Winterset Award and the Metcalf-Rooke Award, and she
has just published a second collection titled *The Freedom in
American Songs*. A long-time resident of St. John's, Newfound-
land, she now lives in Montreal.

Printed in the United States
by Baker & Taylor Publisher Services